To Birdie,

Hoping you enjoy your
New Zealand Christmas.

love & Best wishes,
   Jim & Jan.

December 1977.

Memorial on Mackinnon Pass to its discoverer,
Quintin Mackinnon; Mount Elliott and Jervois
Glacier in background: *Milford*

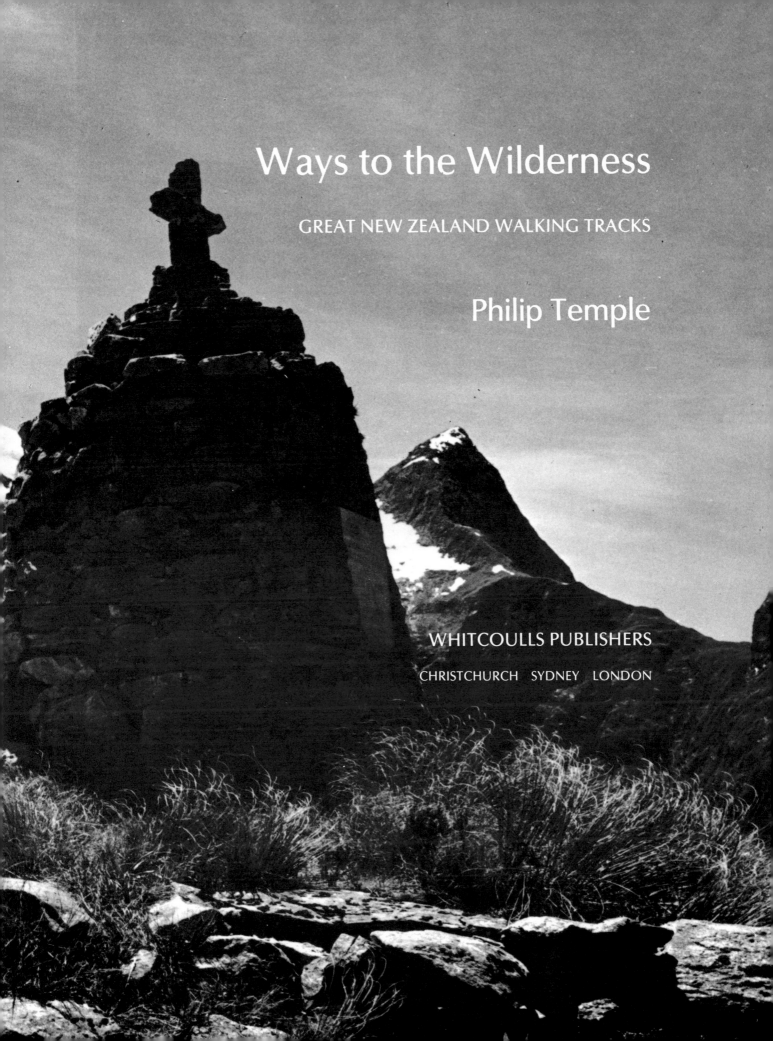

Ways to the Wilderness

GREAT NEW ZEALAND WALKING TRACKS

Philip Temple

WHITCOULLS PUBLISHERS

CHRISTCHURCH SYDNEY LONDON

The giant
buttercup,
*Ranunculus
lyallii:
Routeburn*

CONTENTS

AUTHOR'S NOTE: This is not a guidebook. Anyone who decides to walk any of these tracks should consult other sources for detailed information and advice; in particular the seven Shell Guides (to all but the Rees-Dart Track) which have been issued separately as handy practical companions to this large volume.

PIGEON

First published 1977 © 1977 Philip Temple

Published by Whitcoulls Ltd,
Christchurch, New Zealand

ISBN 0 7233 0537 4

Designed by Philip Temple

Typesetting by Whitcoulls Ltd, Christchurch

Colour separations and printing and binding by Dai Nippon Printing Co. (Hong Kong) Ltd, Hong Kong

INTRODUCTION

IN RECENT YEARS more and more New Zealanders have turned to the unspoilt hills, forests and coasts of our magnificent landscape in search of physical recreation and spiritual solace. Awareness of the value of our natural environment has grown, and shown itself in public efforts to protect it from the often polluting fingers of economic progress. More and more people abandon their cars at the end of long dusty roads and take to the mountains, the river valleys and the bush so that they may discover and appreciate their natural heritage, feel the pulse of the land.

This book is for those who have walked the superb country described and depicted—as a permanent reminder of it—but more especially it is intended as a stimulus to those who wish to begin, to take first steps, regardless of age, into those vast reaches of wilderness that lie beyond the road's end. These eight established walking tracks were chosen because they are within the scope of the relatively inexperienced and may be undertaken by parties including only one or two experienced trampers. They are the safest tracks likely to be found in New Zealand's remote back country, free from major river crossings and well provided with huts.

In sum, the eight tracks traverse an enormous variety of landform and vegetation: lake and volcano, river and canyon, buttercup and rimu, rock and tussock, and always the mountains, the bush and the sea. I was lucky. In gathering the information and taking the photographs for this book and the companion series of Shell Guides I was able to walk all these tracks within two summer seasons. They may take you longer. But everyone is lucky enough, for everyone may, with a little enterprise, embark on the discovery of our unequalled natural landscape.

PHILIP TEMPLE

And this our life, exempt from public haunt,
Finds tongues in trees, books in the running brooks,
Sermons in stones, and good in everything.
                    —WILLIAM SHAKESPEARE, *As You Like It*

WAIKAREMOANA

PARADISE DUCK

Sunrise at Panekiri Hut

Bluffs of the Panekiri Range from Maraunui Bay

Tawa forest
near
Waiopaoa

Korokoro
Falls

View across
Wairau-
moana
from
Panekiri
Range

WAIKAREMOANA, the Sea of Rippling Waters, is set in vast forests redolent of legend and mystery; the land of the Tuhoe, children of the mist, where every tree, rock and stretch of water possessed its own spirit. Proud and warlike, the Tuhoe people in their mountain fastness resisted the attentions not only of other incursive Maori tribes but also of Europeans, long after other parts of the North Island had been settled and cleared. Even today Waikaremoana has the feel of remoteness, for it may be approached only by narrow, winding and unsealed roads from either Wairoa in the east or Rotorua in the west. High up (585 metres) in the unspoilt forest of Urewera National Park, it is a place where one might feel the peace and natural cycles of wind and cloud, water and ancient trees; walk beside rocks and bays and caves invested with the history and lore of the Tuhoe's tangata whenua.

In the distant past, Mahu, the ancestor of many East Coast tribes, lived at Waikotikoti on the shore of Wairaumoana (a bay north of the present lake hut at Waiopaoa). Near by there was a sacred spring where magical rites were performed. Once, Mahu bade his children fetch water to assuage his thirst and all except daughter Haumapuhia went, but inadvertently fetched water from the sacred spring instead of the common one. In a great rage Mahu turned these children into stones, soon to become islets that may still be seen along this shore of Waikaremoana. Then he ordered Haumapuhia to fetch water but she refused to go. Mahu took the water vessel and went himself to the common spring and waited there, resolved to kill his daughter on account of her disobedience. When Hau came to look for her father, he seized her and thrust her under the water until she drowned. Hau was instantly transformed into a taniwha (monster). She forced her way under the earth and tore apart the hills in her effort to escape. First she tried to escape to the north, making a passage until she was stopped by the great Huiarau Range. That was how the Whanganui arm of the lake was created, for the waters of the rivers flowed into channels formed by her struggles. And in her frantic movement she so agitated the surface that from the rippling of the waters the lake derived its name, Wai-kare.

Hau's last attempt to escape was at Te Wharawhara (by the present outlet of the lake at Onepoto). From there she heard the distant murmuring of the sea and made desperate efforts to break through before daylight came, for taniwha may stir only at night. But dawn overtook Haumapuhia and she still lies there in the form of a rock, her head down hill and the waters from the lake running through her body, her hair (kohuwai, a water plant) waving and rippling in the waters.

After Haumapuhia had formed Waikaremoana, she placed a tipua (demon) log in the lake that drifted about its surface for many generations. It drifted across the waters of the lake from place to place, singing strange songs as it moved, songs that were heard and acquired by the men of old. Sometimes the demon log drifted ashore and if anyone interfered with it, misfortune assailed them; next morning the log would be gone. An old Tuhoe man at the turn of the century said: 'I myself heard Tutaua, the log demon, singing far out upon the waters, singing in a strange voice like the whistling of the wind.' Another recalled: 'That demon log drifted out of the lake through the outlet at Te Wharawhara in the days of my youth, drifted away, singing as it went.'

The Tuhoe people trace their origins to the marriage of Rangi-ki-tua, a descendant of Toi, chief of the ancient Maoris who first occupied the Urewera, and Wairaka, daughter of Toroa, captain of the *Mataatua* canoe which arrived at the Bay of Plenty in the fourteenth century. Their grandson was Tuhoe Potiki and he gave his name and prestige to all those who inhabited the cold and cloudy uplands beyond the fertile bay. 'Our oha (inheritance) comes from Toi; our mana (prestige) from Tuhoe.'

The Tuhoe did not count Waikaremoana as part of their tribal lands until the 1820s. Until that time it belonged to the Ngati Ruapani, an East Coast tribe. The Ruapani provoked hostilities about 1823 when they killed two Tuhoe at Hopuruahine (at the head of Whanganui Inlet) and desecrated a chief's body. The Tuhoe warriors, tough and aggressive from generations of hard living in the inhospitable Urewera, retaliated by attacking and defeating the Ruapani at their pas in Whanganui arm. This was the beginning of a war which lasted several years, the primary Tuhoe motive being utu (revenge) for the Ruapani slaughter of women and children while Tuhoe warriors were absent in 1824. By 1830 the Tuhoe had complete domination over Waikaremoana and repelled all invasion attempts by East Coast tribes. The Ruapani were broken and scattered, though some remained through intermarriage. A final peace was made in 1863 and the descendants of Ruapani, with Tuhoe blood in their veins, were once more able to cross at will the arms and valleys of Haumapuhia.

The Tuhoe, because of their isolation from the coast, had little contact with Europeans and long retained a deep suspicion of the invading pakeha. They had almost nothing to trade with either—little flax and few pigs—and in 1830 bought their first musket from Ngati Maru in the Thames district in exchange for ten slaves. The first white men to see Waikaremoana and explore the forests of the Urewera were missionaries, probably the Rev. Father Claude Baty and the Rev. William Colenso, both in December 1841. There was sporadic missionary activity over the subsequent years, and a Church Mission was established at Te Whaiti in 1847. But this was withdrawn in 1852 and there was no resident mission of any church in the Urewera between that time and 1917.

The spread of the Hauhau cult and rebellion against the pakeha in the 1860s brought the Tuhoe into their first conflict with Government troops. In the heart of Tuhoe country, at Ruatahuna, it was decided to meet the enemy at a distance rather than wait until tribal lands were invaded. A war party was sent to assist the Waikato tribes but suffered severely in the defeat at Orakau in 1864. After this, occasional Tuhoe raids were made on towns adjacent to the Urewera, until the notorious rebel Te Kooti escaped from captivity on the Chatham Islands in 1868 and sought refuge in the great forested valleys. Aided and abetted by Tuhoe warriors, Te Kooti fought a running battle with Government troops for more than two years. At this time the Armed Constabulary Redoubt at Onepoto was established, the remains of which can be seen today at the start of the Lake Track. The Government troops employed a ruthless scorched earth policy in their pursuit of the Tuhoe and it is estimated that in October 1870 over 200 people died in Ruatahuna alone from hardship, disease and starvation. By April 1871 the Tuhoe had suffered enough and decided to render allegiance to the Government. But Te Kooti never gave in and, despite many close calls, finally escaped to the King Country where he was pardoned in 1883.

Distrust and dislike of the pakeha remained intense, and surveyors, road builders and census-takers met with suspicion and hostility. Even as late as 1895 it was felt necessary to send troops to protect Government surveyors from possible attack. The Tuhoe were eventually convinced that survey would leave their lands untouched and that road-building would ultimately bring trading and agricultural benefits. By 1891 a road had been constructed into the Urewera from the west as far as Te Whaiti and reached Ruatahuna in 1901. The road from Wairoa reached Waikaremoana in 1897; but the complete through route was not finished until 1930.

As road access improved, pressure increased for milling and farming development of the Urewera. But the disastrous effects of removing forest cover from the unstable country east of Waikaremoana were already plain and economic development was forestalled. As early as 1925 the value of the area as a reserve for climatic and water conservation purposes was realised, as well as its possible designation as a national park to preserve in perpetuity these last great stands of North Island forest for scientific and recreational use.

The hydro-electric scheme at the outlet of Waikaremoana was begun in 1923 and developed over subsequent years, but other economic pressures were successfully resisted as Government sought to bring more and more of the Urewera forests under Crown reserve. Support for the establishment of a national park grew rapidly after World War II and in 1954 the Urewera National Park was officially gazetted. By 1961, when the first park board was appointed, the park had reached nearly 200,000 hectares in extent, second only in size to the Fiordland National Park.

Over the past decade or more the popularity of the park, and of Waikaremoana in particular, has been shown by the thousands of fishermen, trampers, hunters and boatmen who visit the area annually. Throughout the park new tracks have been cut and old Maori trails improved, with huts provided at logical intervals. The project to provide a track around the southern and western margins of Waikaremoana—those not served by the road—was begun in the 1960s and completed in 1970, largely through the efforts of parties of schoolboy volunteers from various parts of the North Island. Now, with five comfortable huts, the tramper can spend three, four or even more days on this 43-kilometre walk, around a lake and through a forest that in combination have no parallel in New Zealand.

∾∾∾

Where you begin the Lake Track depends on whether you approach Waikaremoana from east or west. But if you come up from Wairoa via the cleared valley of the Waikaretaheke, there is incentive to begin immediately, where the road finishes its steep climb and suddenly breasts on to the edge of the lake and the bush of the national park. This is Onepoto where Maori legend avers that the head and shoulders of the petrified taniwha block the outlet of Waikaremoana; but where geologists explain that a massive earthquake-induced landslip blocked the valley behind, like a natural dam, and caused it to fill with water. On the lake bed there are the stumps of a drowned forest and this remains Maori land, leased to the national park.

The lake is at a height of 585 metres, and the site of the Armed Constabulary Redoubt—at the start of the track—lies some sixty metres higher. Here the climb begins, along the crest of the massive sandstone cliffs of Panekiri Bluff, up 532 metres to the Pukenui trig station at 1177 metres, almost the highest point of the track. The climb is steady and relentless, though there is satisfaction in knowing that once these first few hours of effort are done there is no more climbing of significance during the remainder of the walk around the lake.

Red and sometimes silver beech, gnarled and interlocked, dominate the forest canopy which sweeps away on the left hand, down steadily to the lower altitudes beyond the park boundary, southwards to the cleared and eroding hills of northern Hawke's Bay. Periodically, the track breaks through to the edge of the huge rock bluffs on the right hand and one stares down 400 metres to the wrinkled surface of the lake and the white snail wakes of fishing launches headed for the best spots in Wairaumoana or Whanganui Inlet. But if the day is wet and cloudy—and with up to 2500 mm of rain a year this might be the case—then one will look down to a bottomless pit of grey mist, writhing up the layered rocks with the wind, lacing the mossy arms of the ancient trees.

Views out across the main body of the lake, and later towards the northern arms and the Huiarau Range, provide a welcome contrast to the passage of the track through the beech forest. At the edge of the bluffs there is sky and sun or cloud and an impression of space and elevation, and always a scurrying wind. Down thirty metres into the forest there is shelter but a damp gloom in the understorey of saplings and seedlings, grasses and ferns. And a deep silence that is unaccountable until one realises that there is no moving water—no streams, no waterfalls here, high on the crest of the range. The rustling of trees in a wind is welcome and the occasional cheep and chatter of fantail, tomtit and grey warbler, or the rare chiming tones of a hidden tui.

There is no visible end to the undulating track, which reaches a high point of 1225 metres. Then the way seems barred by a rising bluff; but a rock staircase and aluminium ladder lead up to the last stretch of trees before the Puketapu trig and the nearby park hut. Here the forest has been cleared in a swathe back from the edge of the Panekiri cliffs. To the north the many inlets and bays of the lake are set in unblemished arms of forested spurs and hills, green-black trees rolling as far as the eye can see. To the south a scene almost of disaster where the hills have been laid bare by felling and burning; everywhere the land is ravaged by the white scars of erosion, unstable land crumbling without the natural support of root and branch. The view south is better at night when the devastation is hidden and there is some charm in the distant twinkling lights of Wairoa. Even in cloudy weather a stay at Panekiri Hut is worth while, simply to watch sunrise or sunset colours on the fingers of mist that seem to rocket up the cliff face in a westerly wind.

From this hut there is further travel along the crest of the range, an hour or more of gentle descent. Then a right-angle turn to the north brings steep descent, down, down, down, ferreting a way through the bluffs to the gentler hectares of forest that slope from the foot of the uplifted range to the Wairaumoana arm of the lake. Slippery here; awkward there, a branch for support, exposure here where the bluff has slipped away and felled the trees, leaving bare rock for footing. But height is lost quickly and a final drop over a rock slab brings a sudden change in gradient, a sudden change in the forest, for now the beech trees are varied with the drooping traceries of rimu. There is miro too and a thickening undergrowth of small trees and ferns. The forest seems lighter and more expansive, the track broad and well graded, and in the lower regions by the lake, tawa appear, tree ferns and the ubiquitous white-flowered kamahi. Birdlife increases and changes—more tuis, fat pigeons, waxeyes and blackbirds. And slowly, growing in volume, the noise of rushing water as streams on either hand course their way to the sea of rippling water.

At the Waiopaoa Hut one reaches the moving waters of Lake Waikaremoana, which, from this point on, remains constantly on the right hand during the second half of the walk. It is seen through shifting toetoe where deep, dark streams issue into the lake; through the screening margin of manuka; through the podocarp forest or close at hand from rocky headlands. As the track meanders round the shores of Wairaumoana, the view steadily widens until the full span of the Panekiri Range is visible to the south—a notch in the bush at the top indicating the high hut site—and the eastern reaches of the lake can be seen through the Straits of Manaia, as far as Rosie Bay. A feature of the track is the regular diversions it makes up narrow grassy valleys, to bridge crossings where the side streams narrow between gorges of tall trees. These are the haunt of paradise ducks, which, along with shags, herons, shoveller ducks, black teal and mallard, make up the bird population of the lake. Overhead, the lonely harrier hawk, black-backed gull and even the invading, aggressive magpie.

An hour or so along the track from Waiopaoa Hut there is the turnoff to Korokoro Falls. These are worth a side excursion, the track winding by a stream to the 20-metre-high curtain of water cascading evenly and delicately over a sheer rock face. Beyond the turnoff the main track climbs fifty metres or so above the lake, well graded through forest which is a welcome change from the manuka and fern of the lake's edge.

In the day that may be spent in walking from Waiopaoa Hut to Te Puna Hut, the prevailing westerly wind can bring rapid changes in temperature and light: sun and gloom, or the dappled light from broken cloud that lends character and colour to always forested hills. Black overcast and rain can change to sunlight and warmth in the space of half an hour and only in early morning or evening can one expect the lake surface to be entirely still. Rain or sun, forest or lake shore, the mood is always of tranquillity, a sense of timelessness and age.

Three hours from Waiopaoa the track descends once more to the manuka of the shore in Maraunui Bay. Here private huts mark the site of one of several reserves of Maori land, all associated with old pa sites of 150 years ago. This is a secluded corner of the lake, good for fishing and swimming, where the track crosses Whakaneke Spur to Marauiti and another comfortable park hut. Beyond the hut, the track moves from a generally northward trend to the northeast, across the headland between Te Kopua and Te Totara bays, from deep water to forest where occasional totara mix with the rimu and miro. Towards Te Puna the track sticks close to the shore, past Patekaha Island, an island no more with the fluctuations of the lake level caused by the hydro scheme. In all the forest there are signs of possum and deer; often it seems too open, where the seedlings which should grow to replace the aging forest giants have been grazed by the prolific animal blight. In the autumn mating season the quiet of the evening may be punctuated by the distant bellow of red deer bulls.

The final stage of the walk from Te Puna Hut begins with a climb, up and over the neck of land that forms a high forest screen between the secluded remoteness of Wairaumoana and the edge of encroaching civilisation marked by the road and its vehicles on the eastern side of Whanganui Inlet. Though these mean the end of the track and break the natural spell of weather, water and forest under which one has moved during the preceding days, the forest and lake still hold sway and reveal a final pleasure in bending kowhai, yellow blossoms in the spring. From the hut at the head of the Inlet, the last hours' walking allow time to both adjust to old routines that wait at the end of the road and to savour a walking experience that will have proved a source of physical and spiritual enjoyment.

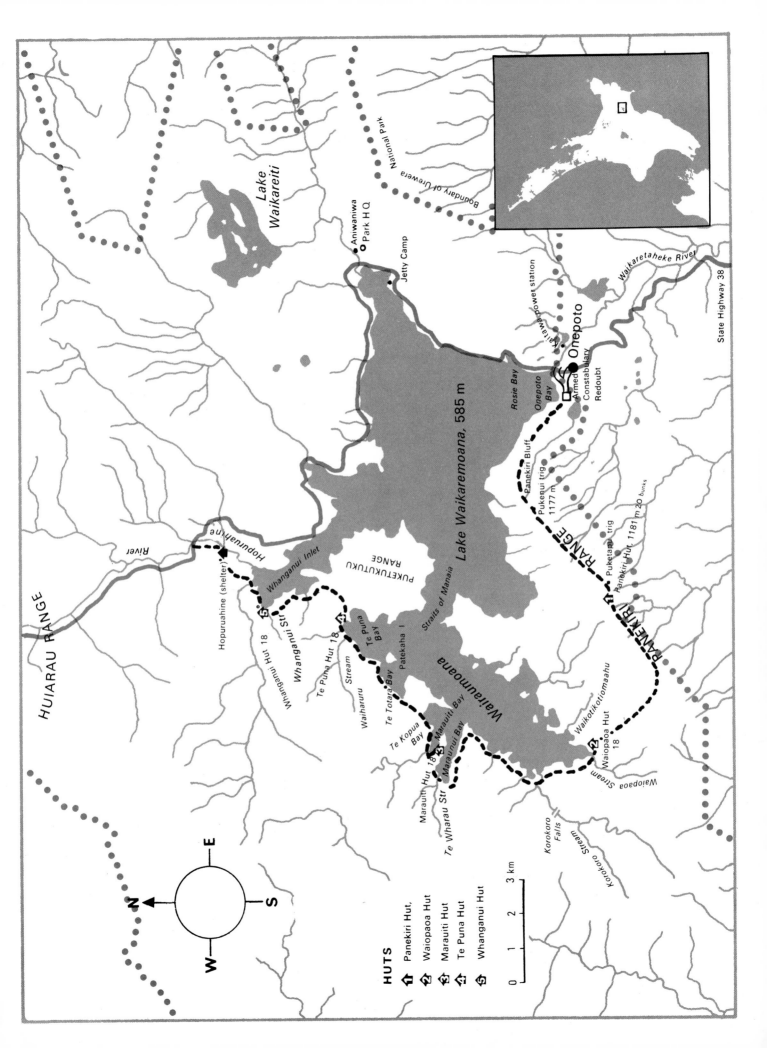

Rimu forest near Te Puna

Panekiri Bluff and Onepoto from head of Whanganui Inlet

Wairaumoana from Waiopaoa

Tapuaenui Bay, Whanganui Inlet

TONGARIRO

PIPIT

Head of the Whakapapaiti Valley, Ruapehu

View west over shrub fields, slopes of Ruapehu

Mangatepopo, Pukekaikiore and Hauhungatahi from the slopes of Red Crater

32

Blighted beech trees
Whakapapait

The
Silica
Springs

A WALK across Tongariro National Park gives the traveller an unparalleled opportunity to see the character, understand the landforms and feel the pulse of New Zealand's great volcanic upland. The scene from the peaks of Tongariro itself has no equivalent on any other track: the rounded sheet of Taupo to the north (New Zealand's largest lake), its water masking the source of violent eruption, reflecting Maori custom and legend. To the south, the primeval scene of Ngauruhoe's black smoking crater, the snow-softened summits of Ruapehu (the North Island's highest mountain), and about them, a ravaged volcanic desert, softened in the west by smoothing tussock and, further, the dark shades of beech forest. This is the most continuously high of the tracks. Though the Copland track tops 2000 metres at the pass, it also drops to fifty metres in the valley; traverse Tongariro and nowhere save at the very end will you drop below 1100 metres in height. Perhaps more than on any other track, there is a feeling of remoteness from the sea, the only clue of it on a clear day—shining Egmont in the west.

That's where it began, a quarrel between Egmont (Taranaki) and Tongariro, the name which once described all the volcanoes of the present national park. In the legendary past Egmont stood between Ngauruhoe and Ruapehu, and to the north, where Lake Rotoaira now lies at the foot of Pihanga, there were two other warriors—Tauhara and Putauaki (Mount Edgecumbe). All sought the hand of soft Pihanga, draped in green forest robes; and their adulation filled the skies with fire, their passion shook the earth. Rivalry grew intense until there was a great battle and for many days and nights the giants raged, spewing forth lava and exploding rock until there remained a sole victor—Tongariro. John Te H. Grace in *Tuwharetoa* writes: 'He became the Supreme Lord over the land and the proud husband of Pihanga. In the days that followed he became the Sacred Mountain of Taupo; his handsome face captured the hearts of all; and he became the possessor of the highest tapu. The eyes of the newborn were directed towards him, and those of the departed rested full upon him as they went their way to the Gathering Place of the Souls.'

The defeated volcanoes had to make their journey of escape under the cover of a single night. When the sun rose first after the cataclysmic battle, Egmont had reached the coast of the setting sun, scouring out the path of the Wanganui River on the way. Edgecumbe stood close by the Bay of Plenty, and now dominates the town of Kawerau. But Tauhara dragged his feet, casting disconsolate glances behind at his lost Pihanga, and remained forever where he might see her across the lake, rising above the town of Taupo.

The name Tongariro derives from the story of Ngatoroirangi, navigator of the *Arawa* canoe and tohunga who travelled inland to claim the Taupo region for his people, the Tuwharetoa. Near the mountains he met a rival claimant for the land, Hapekituarangi. To outwit him, Ngatoro swiftly climbed the flanks of the first mountain to command a wider view of the land. He called down to Hape: 'Do not dare to climb this mountain. If you do I will cause the darkness of the heavens to descend upon you!' Hape ignored him, and Ngatoro called on the volcano god Ruaimoko to destroy his rival. A great storm came up, gale, sleet and snow, and Hape perished in the intense cold. But the cold beset Ngatoro, too, as he pushed on to the summit of the mountain to lay claim to all the land that he could see below. Weak and distressed from the strenuous climb and the bitter cold, he called out to his ancestral spirits and sisters in far off Hawaiki to send fire to warm his chilled body. It came underground, bursting forth as it travelled at White Island, Rotorua, Tarawera and Taupo. As it came nearer, Nga-toro killed a slave, Ngauruhoe, as a sacrifice to the gods and when he cast down a sacred stone on the mountain and the volcano burst into life, he threw the slave's body into the crater. The cold south wind (Tonga) was seized (riro) by the flames.

Tongariro was the sacred mountain for the Tuwharetoa people. Chiefs were buried in its caves and travellers beside the volcanoes spoke in whispers and covered their eyes so that they might not look upon the mountains and offend the gods who dwelt there. The first European travellers in the area were warned not to violate the tapu of Tongariro and any pakeha proposal to climb the volcanoes was greeted with dismay and censure. But John Carne Bidwill, a botanist and explorer who arrived from Sydney early in 1839, showed little concern for the consequences of breaking Maori tapu. He scrambled alone to the top of Ngauruhoe on 3 March, leaving his Maori porters behind. This was both the first ascent of the volcano and the first ascent of any mountain in New Zealand. 'The crater was the most terrible abyss I have ever looked into or imagined . . . It was impossible to get (in) . . . as all the sides I saw were, if not quite precipitous, actually, overhanging so as to make it very disagreeable to look over them. I did not stay at the top so long as I could have wished because I heard a strange noise coming out of the crater which I thought betokened another eruption.'

Maori tapu deterred would-be volcano climbers for many years and Governor Sir George Grey, when he made the first ascent of one of Ruapehu's peaks in 1853, felt obliged to remain hidden from the sight of the Maori companions he had evaded below. By the 1880s Maori influence over pakeha invaders had waned; the fangs of superstition had been drawn by the increasing number of geologists, botanists and amateur explorers who scratched at the flanks and summits of the volcanoes. The eruptions of Ngauruhoe and the contrary habits of Rua-pehu's crater lake were observed with wonder but with increasing scientific detachment. Yet for the descendants of Ngatoroirangi, Tongariro would always be theirs: 'Tongariro is the mountain; Taupo is the lake; Tuwharetoa is the tribe; Te Heu Heu is the man.'

In 1886 Tuwharetoa ownership of Tongariro lands was threatened by the claims of other tribes who had been more loyal to the pakeha Crown in the Land Wars. The Tuwharetoa paramount chief Te Heu Heu IV Horonuku, as Maori patriot, had even assisted the notorious Te Kooti. At Land Court hearings 'loyalist' tribes spoke of the Tuwharetoa as rebels who occu-pied land that should be redistributed among themselves. In order to restore his prestige as a great rangatira in the eyes of Maori and pakeha alike, Horonuku's son-in-law, Lawrence Grace, then Member of Parliament for Tauranga, suggested that he make a gift of the Tongariro volcanoes to the Crown, to be protected in perpetuity as a national park. This would also stifle the claim of rival landowners. In 1887 the gift was made and an act of Parliament in 1894 created New Zealand's first national park.

Creation of a national park did not bring the rapid provision of huts, tracks and rangers. To most New Zealanders of that time the Tongariro region was remote and inaccessible. Although the Desert Road from Waiouru to Tokaanu was complete by 1894, the main trunk railway did not reach the region until 1909 and there was still no road access around Lake Taupo when the first effective park board began operation in 1922. The first major tracks to be formed in the park led to huts established at Waihohonu in the east and Ketetahi on the northern flank of Tongariro in 1903 and 1901 respectively. Tourists who wished to bathe in the Ketetahi Springs or explore the Tongariro craters could take horses up the bridle path from Papakai pa. The remains of this earliest track still form a section of the park traverse described here.

The railway brought most visitors to the western side of the park. A track and hut were put in the Mangatepopo Valley in 1918 for skiers and climbers of Ngauruhoe; in 1920 a dray road was pushed through the forest of the Whakapapa Valley, which became the site of a popular tourist camp before the imposing Chateau Hotel was built in 1929. Much of the early recreational activity and development of the park can be attributed to keen skiers. The Ruapehu Ski Club was established as early as 1913 and in 1923 its members performed the prodigious feat of building a hut at 1768 metres on the Whakapapa slopes—the beginning of the great ski-field developments which now cater for thousands of daily visitors at the height of the winter season.

The face of Tongariro National Park changed dramatically during the 1950s and 1960s. Huts, lodges and ski tows burgeoned above the Chateau, roads were sealed and in 1963 the Ohakune Mountain Road was opened to reach an eventual height of 1585 metres, matching the height of the Bruce Road on the Chateau side of what, the North Island over, had come to be known as 'The Mountain'. As visitor numbers increased by 500 per cent between 1954 and 1971 (373,000 during the latter year), park board rangers struggled to keep pace. Much time and effort went into providing facilities and service for skiing visitors; but a programme of track maintenance and extension was begun and the replacement of huts around the entire park. By the time the Ohakune Mountain Road was opened it was possible to walk with safety and shelter across the entire length of New Zealand's first and most dramatic national park.

∞∞

Begin in the south, gaining all early height up the Ohakune Mountain Road, saving the climax of the 64-kilometre walk—the Tongariro craters—until the end. In the evening perhaps, leave the road at about 1400 metres and drop into the first of the many deep gullies that scour the laval flanks of Ruapehu, the source of rivers that flow 150 kilometres or more into the Tasman Sea—for this is the apex of the North Island's watershed. From the spur beyond, look up towards the highest peak of the mountain at 2797 metres, down to the gently sloping forest slopes and out, out to the convoluted ranges of the King Country and Wanganui.

Now the track drops steeply into the bed of the Mangaturuturu River, through a waterfall of white, frozen lava, perhaps reddish now in the setting sun, evoking memories of the last eruption of lava from the volcano in 1945. The Mountain is mostly quiet, but never dormant. Periodically there is explosive activity in the crater lake. Sometimes enormous mud flows, lahars, caused by melting of Ruapehu's glacial ice, rush down the narrow valleys seaming the mountainside, carrying away all in their path. But if the evening is clear, Egmont beside the setting sun will occupy your thoughts more than lahars—and the slippery footing of the rocks beside the river—until a wet plateau of pumice and scrub is reached, sloping down to the Mangaturuturu Hut, cosseted by the first margin of stunted beech trees.

Begin the next long stage early. It is a tiring section of the Round the Mountain Track; the footing is sometimes rough as the track undulates over open spurs and down into gullies. The way is well marked with white poles at 30-metre intervals. On a sunny day they may seem superfluous, but in mist, rain or hail, which may suddenly blow in from the west on these exposed slopes, they are a comfort and sure guide. From the hut the track meanders through scrub to striking basalt cliffs at the side of the valley. Then it climbs, insinuating steeply through boulders, boggy clearings, moss-covered mountain beeches which despite their dwarfed size may be centuries old. In early morning the mist may be heavy, drifting, dripping through the branches, seeming to deepen the silence which may be broken only by the muffled cheep of pipits. Suddenly one walks out of the trees almost into aptly named Lake Surprise, a high dark tarn. And perhaps now the mist will break and the many shoulders of Ruapehu will be revealed, snow-mantled in autumn, spring and winter.

The track climbs higher still, through luxuriant scrub and the flowers of subalpine vegetation. The forest is left below and the track begins the awkward traverse of the mountain, northwards at a height of more than 1500 metres. Now it lies entirely above the trees, though beech shelter in the gullies is never far below. In sunshine Lake Surprise is blue, a keystone to the vast uninterrupted view ranging over more than 100 degrees of the horizon from south-west to northwest—forest and hills, occasional patches of cleared land and always lonely, banished Egmont. Scoria and boulders beside the track, cliffs and bluffs rearing above, warm with their volcanic reds and browns and greys. Silence save the perpetual noise, sometimes close, sometimes far, of streams and waterfalls which everywhere erode the flanks of the old volcano. In summer the colours of the rocks are added to by flowers, yellow, white and blue, nestled in the protective matt of tough scrub and spongy moss. This is not country for winter travellers, where snow lies deep on the short days with their threat of southerly storm.

After some hours one loses count of the streams and riverheads. There are two branches of the Manganui a te Ao, seven of the Makatote. Only the growing scale of the alpine landscape indicates that the big valleys of the Whakapapa slopes of the mountain are close. With relief one looks down from the last interminable spur to the forked valley of the Whakapapaiti. On the far side there is the choice of steep scoria and exit to State Highway 48 at the Top o' the Bruce. More rewarding is the turn to the left and a short descent, to trees once more, a sparkling stream and a comfortable hut's shelter before the last stage to the Chateau.

For half an hour's travel below the Whakapapaiti Hut the track drops down valley, crossing and recrossing the river over swing bridges, sheltered by the beech-covered spurs on either hand. Above the second bridge, there is a startling view down into the river's gorge, before the track turns 90 degrees to the northeast and the forested traverse to park headquarters. Two hours of forest, the thickest and most varied to be encountered on the Tongariro track. Big beech trees, in some areas gaunt and lifeless from the attack of an unknown blight; kaikawaka (mountain cedar), red and gnarled, blue-green foliage forming its distinctive conical shape;

toa toa (celery pine); broadleaf, five finger and the leathery-leaved mountain cabbage tree. Bird numbers increase—rifleman, grey warbler, silvereye, fantail and tomtit, to replace the lonely pipit and circling harrier hawk of the uplands.

Not far from the Chateau the surface of the track improves. This is the region of shoe tracks and nature walks; labels identify trees and other plants and a sign at a junction points the way south to the Silica Springs—a worthwhile excursion if there is an hour or more to spare. Always there are views to the west down stream beds and now the first sight of steaming Ngauruhoe.

The Chateau is suddenly reached. Over a bridge and there is motor camp, sealed road, park headquarters, garage, grand hotel. Half way; and the sybarite might sneak into cafe or bar; but hard road and angular building seem foreign after two days on the track; and there are eleven kilometres to be covered before nightfall, across the open country beyond.

For the highway is almost a sharp dividing line between forest and tussock. There is more stunted beech close to the Chateau but then scrub and tussock as far as the eye can see, rolling beneath the dominating cone of Ngauruhoe, smoke pouring from its summit at 2291 metres. The firm and even track is a relief after its contortions of the past days, broken only by narrow flood gullies, often dry. Pipit and harrier hawk are at home, as well as black-backed gulls and, rarely, the diving falcon. Continuous views to the western hills; and Ruapehu lies in better perspective with its litter of ski tows and huts; marker poles dwindle into the distance over the rolling tussock; behind the Chateau and ahead, always, Ngauruhoe.

The name of the stream and its adjacent hut underlines the latent power of destruction in the volcanoes above—Mangatepopo, the Stream of Death. Mostly the smoke and steam of Ngauruhoe blow silently away in the westerly wind. But the scars of petrified streams on its flanks testify to the recent flow of molten rock; the litter of clinkery boulders to explosive eruption that may begin at any time. The track now barely skirts the volcano's outpourings, up valley beside the stream, then climbing steeply over lava tongue and clinker to the high saddle between Ngauruhoe and the various peaks of Tongariro. Moving forward from the saddle, one enters a dead, lunar landscape, the South Crater. The surface is smooth and cindered—like a speedway track—with scattered rocks tossed out by explosions; a cockpit between the great volcanoes, a neutral ground.

From the far side of the South Crater the poled route climbs further and from its edge one obtains the first view of the eastern regions of the national park, wilderness and desert and the sculptured landscape of Oturere Crater. The climb continues to the highest point of the track at 1820 metres, the edge of the Red Crater, a surreal world of black mantle, scarlet dike, steaming fumaroles over yellowed rock and, at the northern edge, the small but brilliantly coloured Emerald Lakes. An hour's side trip would lead to the highest peak of Tongariro but the main track leads down sliding cinders beside the very edge of Red Crater to the lakes and the kilometre-wide Central Crater. At its far side is Blue Lake; but in all these wild sculptures and vivid colours Ngauruhoe looms like a dark Nemesis, smoking quietly before the next violent shrug of subterranean forces.

From the saddle at the northern side of Central Crater the last stage of the track is in sight and soon, following the easy zigzag down, a sweeping view to the north opens out—Lake Rotoaira, fair Pihanga and great Taupo. Rough rock gives way to tussock and further down it is worth a night's stay at Ketetahi Hut to take in the incomparable sunset light over the lakes, and the luxury of a bathe in the nearby hot springs.

The last downhill kilometres of the track take an hour or two—tussock spurs at first, gently steaming from the influence of the adjacent springs. Then swiftly and steeply into the forest; thin-barked totara, cabbage tree, toa toa, haven for pigeon and bellbird. And lower, where the gradient eases and the track wriggles by fast running creek and waterfall, the moist and shady forest is haven for the traveller, after wind- or sun-blasted heights redolent of powerful, earth-making forces; latent natural cataclysm.

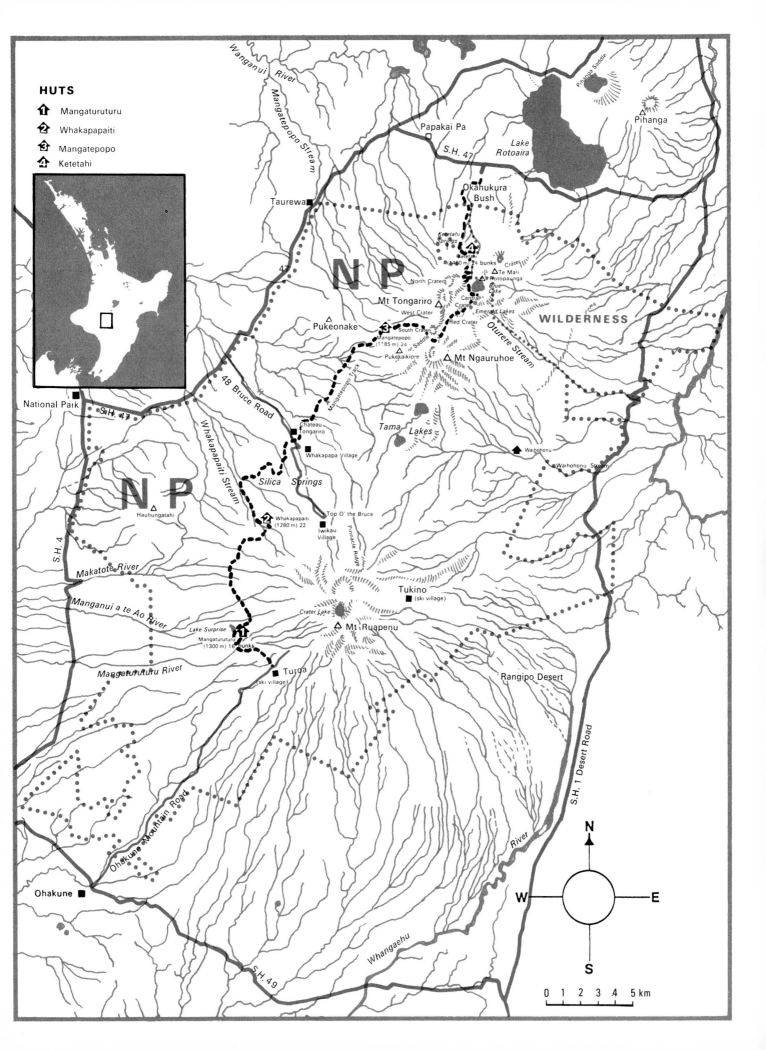

HUTS

1 Mangaturuturu
2 Whakapapaiti
3 Mangatepopo
4 Ketetahi

Wanganui River

Mangatepopo Stream

Papakai Pa

S.H. 47

Lake Rotoaira

Pihanga Saddle

Pihanga

Taurewa

Okahukura Bush

Ketetahi Springs

Ketetahi
(1460 m) 24 bunks

N P

Te Mari
Rotopaunga

Crater

North Crater

Blue Lake

Mt Tongariro

West Crater

Central Crater

WILDERNESS

Pukeonake

3
Mangatepopo
(1185 m) 24

South Crater

Emerald Lakes

Red Crater

Oturere Stream

Saddle

Pukekaikiore

Mt Ngauruhoe

National Park

S.H. 47

48 Bruce Road

Whakapapaiti Stream

Mangatepopo Track

Chateau Tongariro

Whakapapa Village

Tama Lakes

Waihohonu

Waihohonu Stream

N P

Hauhungatahi

Silica Springs

Top O' the Bruce

2
Whakapapaiti
(1280 m) 22

Iwikau Village

Pinnacle Ridge

S.H. 4

Makatote River

Manganui a te Ao River

Lake Surprise
Mangaturuturu
(1300 m) 16 bunks

1

Crater Lake

Mt Ruapenu

Tukino
(ski village)

Rangipo Desert

Mangaturuturu River

Turoa
(ski village)

Ohakune Mountain Road

S.H. 1 Desert Road

River

Ohakune

S.H. 49

Whangaehu

N

W — E

S

0 1 2 3 4 5 km

Lichen, *Cladonia* sp.

Gentian, *Gentiana* sp.

Umbrella fern, *Gleichenia cunninghamii*

White daisy or mountain musk, *Celmisia incana*

Ngauruhoe and Pukekaikiore from the Mangatepopo Track

Moss and mountain
beech near
Lake Surprise

Mangaturuturu
Falls

Dyke in Red Crater;
Rangipo Desert in distance

Lake Rotoaira, Pihanga, Taupo and Tauhara, from Ketetahi

47

Emerald Lakes

HEAPHY

ROBIN

Big River on the Gouland Downs; Slate Range beyond

Heaphy River near junction with Lewis River (aerial)

Toetoe beside the Heaphy River

Old rata, Heaphy Valley

The nikau
coast,
north to
Heaphy
Bluff
(aerial)

OF ALL the tracks described here, the Heaphy has received most public attention in recent years, attendant on the controversy about whether the line of the track should be used for a motor road joining Karamea on the West Coast and Collingwood in Golden Bay. Conservationist outcries have stimulated active interest in the track to the point where the annual number of walkers exceeds even that for the Milford Track; and its evident popularity as a walking track was a major factor in Government's move to postpone a decision on road construction for several years.

Ironically, the track has seen heavy use only over the past decade. Though cleared and formed in 1888, it was described as overgrown in 1907 and in 'serious disrepair' in 1931. Though a road has been mooted at regular intervals since the founding of Karamea in 1874, the formed track saw little use even in the days of horse traffic. Modern argument for a road can be seen entirely in the interests of tourist operators who foresee another South Island round trip to include in package coach tour brochures. A through road is unlikely to benefit Karamea or Collingwood, any more than the opening of the Haast Pass benefited the township of Haast in South Westland.

The Heaphy does not lie within a national park, but is encompassed by the North-West Nelson Forest Park, and the Gouland Downs have been a scenic reserve since 1915. Any road proposal must take into account the possibility of damage to the flora and fauna of this unique area and, even more obviously, the destruction of the marvellous nikau coast south of the Heaphy River. Motorists lament the fact that only trampers may view the palm-studded coastline, culminating in the dense nikau and flax groves around the Heaphy River mouth and beaches. Yet construction of a road would inevitably and thoroughly destroy what the motorist wants to see. The unstable rock of the spurs falling steeply to the beaches would slip and scar under the impact of bulldozers; and where the hills relent to admit an easier roadmaking line, the belts of nikau palms are at their thickest. As James MacKay wrote in 1860: 'It would be next to impossible to make a road over these eleven miles of rock and stone beach. . . .'

Charles Heaphy and Thomas Brunner were the first white men to see the nikau coast and the Heaphy River but they did not investigate the Maori route which was said to lead beyond its headwaters to the Aorere Valley and Golden Bay. On 17 April 1846 Heaphy and Brunner —both only 23 years of age—were already a month out of Nelson on their epic four-month exploration of the West Coast which took them from Wanganui Inlet in the north to the Ara-hura River in the south. They had endured terrible physical hardships in traversing the savage coast to the north, rock-climbing down cliffs and bypassing bluffs by wading through the receding wash of giant breakers. Through driving sou'-west rain on 17 April they scrambled through tangled rata and kiekie to the top of Heaphy Bluff and looked down on the river which their Maori guides E Kehu and Enehu called Wakapohai. They told of the old trail to the Aorere and of open land fit for wheat growing where there were also many wekas to be caught. Undoubtedly they referred to the Gouland Downs. The party was forced to travel up the Heaphy valley about two kilometres before a safe ford could be found, but the beaches to the south afforded some of the best travelling that they had encountered. Camp on the evening of 18 April was made at the foot of Kohaihai Bluff, 'a remarkable conical projection of the sandstone rock'. From the saddle on the next morning they looked out to the long sandy beach curving away to the Karamea River, 'and the level country of the same name which lies in the hollow of the bay'.

Heaphy and Brunner reached the great Buller River by the end of April and Heaphy wrote whimsically of the delights and hardships that had marked their journey and which, in fact, characterise the life and surroundings of anyone, even today, who would push into the wilder regions of New Zealand bush and mountain country. 'Go to the bush if you would enjoy the sight of Nature in her loveliest aspect, fresh and beautiful . . . Sleep by the side of the rushing river and dream of its passage in the morning if you would enjoy repose healthful and invigorating. Cross the high mountain, or strike into the dark unexplored forest if you want excitement; and for quiet pleasure, watch the water-fowl on the lake. . . . And should you wish to enjoy a climate unequalled, go to Kawatiri (Buller); build yourself a house six feet long by four; spread your blanket on the ground; dry your clothes by degrees; get blinded by the smoke, drifting with the rain and hail in your eyes; amuse yourself for a week with eating fern-root, and wish yourself comfortably at your coffee and toast by your own fireside in Nelson.'

In 1856 James MacKay and John Clark explored the Aorere Valley from Golden Bay, and from Lead Hill (1610 m), to the east of the upper valley, they looked out to the Tasman Sea beyond rugged bush-covered hills and a wide basin of scrub and tussock. This basin was soon named Gouland Downs after the Collingwood magistrate who applied for it as a stock run, though he dropped the application when he discovered that the downs were useless for grazing.

Four years later, the same James MacKay led a party of unsuccessful gold prospectors from the Buller to Collingwood, substantially over the present route of the Heaphy Track. He submitted a detailed description of the route, noted a coal seam in the lower Heaphy and commented favourably on the gold-bearing prospects of the area. In 1861 gold was found at Karamea and MacKay re-traversed the track with John Knyvett, repeating his comments. As resident magistrate at Collingwood the following year, he pressed for a bridle track to 'open that supposed gold-yielding tract, and also some very fine land in the valley of the Greenfield, and on the northwestern branch of the Heaphy'. No one seemed to share MacKay's view and the route was used only occasionally, even after Karamea's founding in 1874.

The Government Chief Surveyor's report for 1882–3 mentioned work by surveyor C. Lewis in preparing sketch plans for a road 'extending from Gouland Downs on the north to the Lyell Ranges on the south'. And later a line was surveyed from Takaka for a road to join the proposed Collingwood-Karamea track at the Downs. In February 1883 Lewis took a party from Takaka down the Karamea River and returned via the Heaphy route. The difficulty of the country extended an expected three-week survey to five. By the time they reached Gouland Downs the party's provisions were finished. 'Dinner was not a heavy meal as all that we had for the four of us was one crow and one robin, and of these we ate everything except the feathers. We boiled and then divided them, and drank the water they were boiled in, and then roasted the bones brown and ate them, even to the claws and beaks.' The party arrived at Collingwood in rags.

Finally, in 1888, J. B. Saxon surveyed and graded the Heaphy Track for the then Collingwood County Council. But as a line of communication between Karamea and Collingwood it was little used and reports by visiting scientists after the turn of the century all pointed to its overgrown and deteriorating condition. James MacKay's gold had never been found but the unusual range of flora and fauna of the Gouland Downs region was recognised in 1915 by the gazetting of a scenic reserve. At 600 metres above sea level, the Downs contain some of the oldest sedimentary rocks in New Zealand and support a vegetation that includes silver and mountain beech, small totara and large-leafed dracophyllums. Reports of birdlife at regular intervals since 1860 have indicated strange fluctuations in population. A century ago birdlife was reported as being almost non-existent, yet in February 1915 a natural historian estimated a population of about 30,000 wekas and thousands of kiwis. Investigations after a widespread fire over the Downs in 1938 revealed that the area seemed to be lacking in any form of animal life; but twenty years later fourteen different species of birds were reported, with great spotted kiwis and western wekas in abundance. Whatever may explain the rise and fall of bird populations, the Gouland Downs and their surrounding hills and valleys are a rich source of study for both botanist and ornithologist.

The Heaphy became increasingly popular as a tramping track after World War II, though none of its creeks and rivers, dangerous in flood, were bridged and hut accommodation was limited and primitive. In the early 1960s there were huts on the Downs, at Lewis River and at the Heaphy River mouth, but all were small and only the Heaphy was in good repair. A tramper in 1963 described the Lewis Hut as a 'three star hotel. . . . Despite the fact that you either sleep on the floor or outside, that the rain puts the fire out, and that you walk a quarter of a mile for water, it does provide shelter against rain, and a limited space to keep gear out of the reach of wekas.'

But work by the New Zealand Forest Service in the late 1960s and early 1970s, in response to the track's greatly increased popularity, has changed the face of the Heaphy, bringing it up to a standard probably undreamt of by Saxon in 1888. Now, the track is clear, benched and well marked; all the rivers and major creeks are bridged; there are commodious huts on Perry Saddle, Gouland Downs, on the MacKay ridge leading down to the Heaphy River, at the junction of the Lewis and Heaphy and at Heaphy River mouth; there are road-end shelters at either end of the track and emergency shelters at Blue Duck and Katipo creeks. During the summer Forest Service rangers maintain both track and huts and keep a benevolent eye on the motley thousands of walkers. Now the Heaphy Track justifies its cutting nearly ninety years ago, providing a way for people of all ages to experience the life and landscape of the unexploited country in the northwest corner of the South Island; a fine recreational route for the increasing number of walkers who seek a natural refuge from the encroaching tyranny of the motorcar.

∞∞∞

The Heaphy can be walked from either end, but for a first walk over the track there is much to recommend a start from Collingwood. Nearly all the climbing is completed within the first few hours over a graded zigzag through the forest and, from Perry Saddle on, there is a feeling of exploration and anticipation, moving over the Gouland Downs to the headwaters of the Heaphy River and then down to the climax of the trip at the nikaus and beaches of the river mouth.

The road-end in the Aorere Valley is marked by the overnight shelter of Brown Hut and the first of twelve aluminium footbridges which almost entirely remove flood danger for Heaphy walkers. Once over the Brown River the climb begins, over scrubby farmland with views down the unkempt valley towards Collingwood; fern and manuka to the leading spur where the graded track soon shows itself and disappears (a welcome change on a hot day) into the dense bush that dominates the lumpy ranges to the south and west and east. Fern tree and fantail, rimu and robin, beech tree and moss bank fill the hours of climbing, 800 metres to the highest point of the journey over a soft and even trail that swings back and forth so regularly and at such a steady grade that the pattern of walking becomes almost monotonous. But monotony is tempered by the thought that rarely has such an easy path been made up the side of a mountain.

At times the forest becomes oppressive and one is conscious only of the steep slopes climbing, climbing to the unseen convolutions of the ridge-tops; falling, falling to the bed of the Aorere River, more sensed than seen beneath the dense ranks of trees and undergrowth. Clearings through the trees are rare but, before the track finishes its southerly trend and makes its decisive sweep to the west, there is a chance—on a clear day—to see beyond Golden Bay and Farewell Spit to the smoky blue coast of the North Island, terminated by the cone of Mount Egmont. And further on there is a lookout to the headwaters of the Aorere and its source in the 1500-metre Tasman Mountains.

Time and distance may be suddenly reduced by a steep shortcut that goes straight up the hillside, cutting off a wide loop in the track; and after four or five hours travelling a sharp bend and the start of gentle descent mark Flanagan's Corner and the highest point of the Heaphy at 915 metres. Two kilometres more as the bush thins and the track grows both rockier and wetter from oozing streams. Then Perry Saddle and hut, muddy tussocks, bare tops, east the jagged ridge of Anatoki, west the soft curve of spurs masking the promised Gouland Downs.

The track wriggles between the spurs and through the low bush shadowing Perry Creek—down until the spurs fall back, the trees thin into scrub, and then red spiky snowgrass ripples in the wind, masking saturated pakihi. The Downs roll low to the hut at their centre, broken by streams which have cut deep into the limestone, streams like Cave and Shiner Brooks and Weka Creek, all of which go to form Big River draining to the Tasman Sea near the Kahurangi Point light. There are beech forest knolls, rocks and caves which harbour kiwis whose whistles can be heard at night in company with the screech of wekas and the hoots of moreporks. During the day the Downs are likely to be silent, a still moorland, cupped by dark surrounding hills. The steady movement of clouds, and the light shift of snowgrass bring no sound; and the noise of running water in creek beds or the fluctuating call of pipits give relief in a landscape that seems barren and lifeless.

From Downs Hut the track gently climbs and seems to grow muddier by the hour, ploughed by hundreds of passing boots, almost impassable at times after heavy rain, so that it often grows wider where travellers have tried to find firmer ground at the sides. Beyond Weka Creek the climb steepens for a while through scrub; manuka coarse and rasping in the wind, dead trees sculptured and white against the hillside. The bush draws close again and for the next ten kilometres to MacKay Hut the track twists and turns, climbs and then falls steadily through forest and boggy clearings, decorated with boulders and the runnels of rocky streams. From the clearing of Saxon River the track turns north briefly, then makes a final rise to the ancient signpost marking the boundary between Buller and Collingwood counties. Traces of camp fires and the first distant view of the Tasman Sea beyond the mouth of the Heaphy River. Perhaps it is late afternoon now, and there is relief in the steady drop down the ridge, warmth in the clearings where the sun glares off white limestone gravel, cool in the deep shade of trees or where the wind rises from the valley and swirls over the tops. As the sun sets directly into the sea, smoke from MacKay Hut marks the last wide view of the lower valley and the sea.

Below MacKay Hut, named for James MacKay of 1860, the track soon resumes the grade and character that marked the climb from Brown River to Perry Saddle. The forest harbours a humid warmth that is welcome after the chill austerity of the Downs. Rimu and fern trees abound in growth that seems doubly lush after snowgrass and limestone. Birds increase; robins are common, fantails, waxeyes, pigeons and perhaps kakas in the high canopies. But lower down the hills close in to the upper gorge of the Heaphy, and the brown river winding through white beaches catches the eye through rare breaks in the trees. At one point the track turns black where it crosses a coal seam and then, a hundred metres or so above Lewis Hut, the first nikau palms appear and slowly thicken over the last kilometres of the journey to the coast.

On a bright sunny day the river is a brown stain through the nearly black forest, harsh lines and colour; in rain the scene is muted and grey, enlivened only by the crisp contours of nikau and fern tree and the waving straw heads of toetoe. Over the Heaphy bridge the track runs first through forest shade, later beside the river, climbing to negotiate rocks and bluffs, crossing wide tributaries and river beach to the last stretch of trees before the sea. On a dull day the sea reveals its presence by water-reflected light on the belly of the cloud. But on a clear day there is no warning save the final lowering of the hills on either side of the valley and the mile pegs which indicate that Heaphy Hut is close. Suddenly the hut and the lagoon are revealed, the cliffside of Heaphy Bluff, the sand bar and the incomparable sweep of nikaus. A short walk beyond the hut leads to the beach: the confines of forest and valley are forgotten in the huge sweep of the coast to the south, curving 120 kilometres to Cape Foulwind beyond Westport. Beach and rock and bluff, but mostly wide reaches of sand and the incessant surf. A fine evening at the Heaphy River mouth will never be forgotten, when the sun sinks through the horizon clouds to the sea and the severe lines of nikau and flax stand black and stark against the warm sky and the gilded waters of lagoon and ocean.

In the lower Heaphy there may be cattle, and cowpats to snare the barefooted. Further down the coast sandflies may be traded for wasps. But the final leg of the 78-kilometre journey will prove a delight for those more suited to sea and sand than bush and mountain. As the surf pounds through boulders at the rocky points or pulls at the crescent beaches, the high and silent bowl of the Gouland Downs seems a world away. Of the sixteen kilometres from Heaphy Hut to the road-end at the Kohaihai River, about a third must be traversed across open beaches, a dragging business for those more accustomed to hard tracks. But the rest of the trail runs behind the beaches, in the welcome shade of nikaus, regularly crossing streams that drain the gullies; or it cuts across hill faces and points, above the barriers of jumbled boulders or the encroaching line of the sea at high tide.

The long view of the southern coast closes towards Kohaihai Bluff, that 'remarkable conical projection' described by Charles Heaphy. The hedge of flax and nikau grows thinner and there are signs of civilisation in the scattering of huts at Scotts Beach. The bush-covered bluff marks the end of the Heaphy Track. From the saddle at the top of the last gentle climb one sees that the bluff and its skirting tidal river also mark the end to the West Coast road. They are natural barriers that anyone who has walked the Heaphy, and enjoyed its peace and unspoilt character, hopes will never be breached in the short-sighted pursuit of commercial 'progress'.

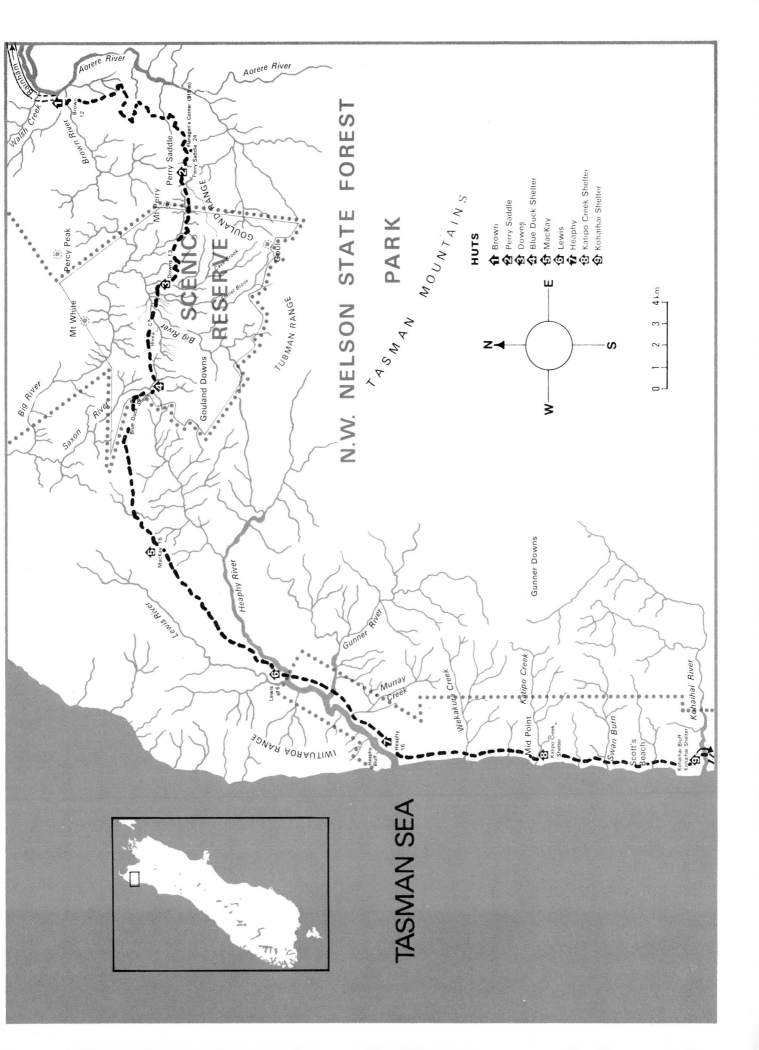

N.W. NELSON STATE FOREST

PARK

TASMAN MOUNTAINS

SCENIC
RESERVE

GOULAND RANGE

TUBMAN RANGE

IWITUAROA RANGE

TASMAN SEA

HUTS

1 Brown
2 Perry Saddle
3 Downs
4 Blue Duck Shelter
5 MacKay
6 Lewis
7 Heaphy
8 Katipo Creek Shelter
9 Kohaihai Shelter

N
W — E
S

0 1 2 3 4 km

Bainham

Walsh Creek

Aorere River

Aorere River

Brown River

Brown
12

Perry Saddle

Flanagan's Corner (915 m)

Perry Saddle 24

Mt Perry

Percy Peak

Mt White

Goulda

Cave Brook

Shiner Brook

Downs 13

Big River

Weka Cr

Big River

Saxon River

Gouland Downs

Blue Duck Shelter

MacKay
16

Lewis River

Heaphy River

Gunner River

Gunner Downs

Katipo Creek

Lewis
16

Heaphy
16

Heaphy Bluff

Murray Creek

Wekakura Creek

Mid Point

Katipo Creek Shelter

Swan Burn

Scott's Beach

Kohaihai Bluff
Kohaihai Shelter

Kohaihai River

Frosted
treetops
at Perry
Saddle;
Anatoki
ridge in
distance

Tree fern
and rimu,
Heaphy
Valley

Headwaters of the Aorere Valley

Dead manuka above Weka Creek

Sunset at the Heaphy rivermouth

Nikaus

COPLAND

KEA

Hot spring, Welcome Flat

Hooker River with Mount Cook beyond

From the climb to the pass; Ben Ohau Range
above mist-shrouded Hooker and Tasman valleys

Copland River below Architect Creek

Daisies at
the head
of the
Copland

ALL THE great names of New Zealand mountain exploration and climbing are associated with the Copland Pass and track, from Charlie Douglas and Arthur Harper to Peter Graham and Freda du Faur to the guides and amateurs of later years. For the Copland is the lowest Main Divide pass between the great alpine region of the Mount Cook district and the bush and glaciers of the West Coast. In the days before ski-planes and fast motor roads it made for the quickest route, albeit on foot, between the tourist centres of the Hermitage and Fox-Franz Josef. And for many years it proved a favourite guided trip for travellers who did not aspire to the heights of 3000-metre peaks but who desired first-hand experience of the alpine environment at the apex of the Southern Alps. Over a distance of nearly fifty kilometres the track takes the traveller from the tussock and moraine, the rock and ice of the Hermitage region to the dense forest, rivers and hot springs of Westland, a vivid contrast in landscape paralleled by the great height differential of the track, the most marked of any included in this book—from 2150 metres at the snow of the Main Divide to only 50 metres above sea level on the flats of the Karangarua River.

In 1892 the Government was anxious to find a route for a tourist road connecting the West Coast with the Mount Cook region and Explorer Charles Douglas was given instructions to discover 'a pass available for Mule traffic to the Hermitage'. Douglas started up the Copland in late March, hacking through virgin bush, scrambling through gorges where boulders 'worn into fantastic shapes by the action of the water' provided 'the best scene on the Copeland for beauty'. But he was glad to reach the open spaces of Welcome Flat, for 'Occasional glimpses of Peaks and Glaciers through dense foliage may be very pretty and verry Artistic but they are aggravating to ordinary mortals.' To the south he saw the Sierra Range, more wonderful to him than Queenstown's renowned Remarkables, 'looking as if some Giant with little skill and a very bad file had attempted to make a saw out of the Mountains'.

Douglas explored first the Strauchon branch of the Copland, noting that there was no way for a road or track across icy and precipitous Baker Saddle, Mount Cook towering beyond. But the head of the Copland offered better possibilities, though 'the immense snow fall in winter at the height the saddle is would obliterate every season any road formation'. His judgment and advice were precise and accurate: 'It would be only used by the more adventurous Alpine travellers. . . . make a foot track—benched where necessary . . . then a few cairns to guide people in a fog . . . A wire bridge over Archetect creek, and an iron hut at either the foot of the saddle or on Welcome flats . . .' The Douglas prescription was to be fulfilled.

In 1895 E. A. FitzGerald of the Alpine Club (London) arrived at the Hermitage with his Swiss guide Mattias Zurbriggen, intending to carry off all the climbing prizes in the district. He was forestalled on Mount Cook by the New Zealand party which had planted a sugar bag on its summit the previous Christmas Day; but he made first ascents of a number of great peaks, including Tasman and Sefton. In late February he determined to make a pass from the Hooker Valley to the West Coast and with Zurbriggen experienced little difficulty in reaching the Main Divide at Fitzgerald Pass (just south of the Copland Pass). He saw 'no difficulty in building a bridle path from the Hermitage'. At the saddle they drank a bottle of wine and, since it was Zurbriggen's patron saint's day they made 'a regular feast' of lunch, 'consuming all our provisions with the exception of a few biscuits, for Zurbriggen said that we could easily reach some habitation early next morning'.

Zurbriggen had boobed, for the pair spent two and a half days struggling through gorge and forest before they encountered a survey party near the site of the present Karangarua road bridge. In the gorge of the Copland they undertook 'a series of acrobatic feats in rock-climbing that would have satisfied the most ardent gymnast' and crawled through 'subterranean caves hollowed out by the action of the water'. Travel in the bush was not much better with its thick undergrowth and twining supplejack. Starving and exhausted, the explorers staggered into Scott's homestead to be greeted by Charlie Douglas and his young mate Arthur Harper. Douglas, old bushman that he was, no doubt cast a jaundiced eye on the pair and their tale of epic struggles in the Copland. But Harper was a fellow Alpine Club member, later a long-serving president of the New Zealand Alpine Club, and offered to accompany FitzGerald and Zurbriggen back to the Hermitage in a first crossing of Graham Saddle at the head of the Franz Josef Glacier.

Harper had been on the point of making the first crossing from the Copland to the Hermitage when the visitors had arrived at Scott's, and he repeated their journey a couple of weeks later, making much lighter work of it. Already FitzGerald's one upmanship in claiming undue credit for mountain exploration and discovery was well known; and after his own crossing, Harper took some of the wind out of his sails. 'The Copland is not . . . a bad river to descend . . . I do not think the route I took . . . would account altogether for the shorter time; it was probably due, to some extent, to my being generally more accustomed to rough work than FitzGerald and Zurbriggen. . . . the times made by these two are good; but the pity of it is that *it was all a waste of energy, owing to their having no means of ascertaining how to tackle this country.*'

Slowly the Copland became a regular route for alpine travellers. Douglas supervised the blazing of a track in the middle 1890s and two of his companions discovered the hot mineral springs at Welcome Flat. In 1897 Malcolm Ross, returning to the Hermitage after his difficult crossing of Whymper Saddle, made the first west to east crossing of the Copland Pass and recorded that parts of the blazed track were already obliterated by slips and fresh forest growth. The way must have been even more overgrown for the first three women to be guided over the pass in 1903.

Later that same year Peter Graham crossed to the Hermitage from his West Coast home to begin his famous career as a guide at Mount Cook. He held the position of chief guide from 1906 to 1922, leading many of the great climbers of his day to first ascents and new routes on the big peaks in the east. He described following the rough track on the north bank of the Copland, which at that time did not cross the river until the upper limit of Welcome Flat. There were no bridges and no huts. '. . . as I had no blankets I collected ferns with the aid of my penknife and was warm and comfortable with a quantity of these above and below me. Wekas visited me more than once during the night.' At the Douglas Rock bivouac at the bush-line he was met by Hermitage guide Jack Clarke—a member of the first party to the summit of Mount Cook—and guided over the pass to his new job.

A year or two later the Public Works Department began construction of a horse track from the Karangarua Flats. Progress was painfully slow but Graham had cause to thank the workmen in 1907. After a near-fatal journey down the Copland when the river and every creek was in raging flood, he came upon their new footbridge across notorious Architect Creek. At the work camp four kilometres further on he found shelter until the floods receded.

In fine weather the crossing of the pass itself caused few difficulties, for the way was clear over rock ridge and snow basins on the highest slopes. By 1910 the way from the Hermitage lay over a new track and footbridges across the Hooker River to a new hut at the foot of the climb to the pass. But Freda du Faur, who made the crossing in February with Otto Frind and Peter Graham, found the upper Copland a scramble through thick scrub and 'tough alpine vegetation'. Earlier, from the pass she had seen 'Far away at the River's mouth a white line marking the waves breaking on the beach. . . . Behind me lay Mount Cook, glistening silver-white in the morning sunshine; cold, cruel, and careless the great peak pierced the sky.' At Architect Creek the party was met by a boy with three horses and they rode to Scott's farm, and on to Fox and Franz Josef the following day. Until World War II there was no motor road south to the Karangarua and a horse trek from Architect Creek to the West Coast glacier hotels was a feature of every Copland crossing.

In 1913, after her second crossing of the Copland, Freda du Faur reported that 'things have been made considerably easier for the tourist. The track now comes right up to the snow-grass, and the old battle through the scrub which was such a waste of time and temper is consequently done away with.' There was still no bridge at Welcome Flat and she was carried across the river to the half-completed hut and the 'Copland Hot Springs' for the luxury of a hot bath. She opined that if the Government 'endeavours to remove the sandflies which are all too active for comfort, these springs should prove a most popular resort'!

Between the wars the Copland grew increasingly popular for 'guided tourists'. The track was steadily improved so that horses could be taken as far as Welcome Flat, where a footbridge was thrown across the Copland. In 1932 a hut was completed near Douglas Rock, a fine natural bivouac since buried by avalanche. The hut was built from totara pitsawn on the site and with other materials backpacked from Welcome Flat. Guide Mick Bowie recalls meeting the overseer of the work, George Bannister, who had been the first Maori to climb Mount Cook twenty years earlier. 'George had a roll of malthoid on his back—100 lb—and treated it like a feather!' Bowie offered to help Bannister but the Maori demurred and moved non-stop from Welcome Flat to Douglas Rock—eight kilometres—where Bowie 'felt as if he had run a marathon!'

After World War II the Copland's popularity waned, coincident with the decline of guiding and the 'new look' in tourism—package coach tours that took in half the South Island at speed and precluded the deeper, if more arduous, delights of a transalpine crossing. The Architect Creek bridge provided a more dangerous crossing than the ford and the Welcome Flat Hut was without bunks and a windowless haven for sandflies.

Reprieve came in 1960 when the Westland National Park was formed to complement the Mount Cook park over the Main Divide. Now the track surface has recovered nearly to the state of earlier days and the huts have been renovated; there are new footbridges and an emergency shelter beneath the pass. Dozens of enterprising trampers use the pass each summer, indulging in the panoramic views of Mount Cook and the acres of subalpine gardens at the head of the Copland River.

∽∾∽

Whether one approaches the Copland Pass from the west or east depends on how one likes to gain height—slowly, steadily and long-windedly up the Copland Valley or quickly and steeply from the Hooker. On a fine day there is probably no view to beat the sudden revelation of Mount Cook on breasting the pass from the west. But most travellers seem to prefer to get the hard work (and pain?) over with quickly and take the long view of a hot bathe in the Welcome Flat pools as therapy for aching muscles.

The track begins beyond the Hermitage, at 760 metres beside the memorial to Sydney King, Darby Thomson and John Richmond, first men to die on Mount Cook in 1914. The mountain looms beyond and, though it is lost to sight for a while, it soon grows more dominant, filling the view of the valley. Walking towards Hooker Hut, the south face appears to grow in size, bulging with hanging ice that sometimes falls in spectacular avalanches. The mountains beside Mount Cook seem puny, subordinate to the massive structure of rock, snow and ice that rises in buttress, shelf and wall, 2500 metres above the valley floor.

At first the track winds through moraine hillocks, crossing and recrossing the Hooker River by swing bridges; at times the track is carved from solid rock or supported by man-made platform, grey rapids beating through the boulders below. Mount Sefton commands the Main Divide to the west, but its cliffs and ice faces are slowly lost to view as one travels up the valley, until its summit is seen end on, sharp and graceful, underlined by its aptly named partner, the Footstool.

Beyond the swing bridges there are flats and terraces beside the river and if you walk in early summer, giant mountain buttercups—the famous Mount Cook lily—glisten among the tussocks and rocks, soft and delicate relief in a landscape composed largely of grey scree and moraine, brown buttress and glaring ice. There may be banks of snowberries, hebes, gentians and golden spaniard too; but except in the brief climax of flowering, plant life seems as awed by the harsh alpine environment as the sweating traveller.

Beyond the lunch hut, the track winds and rises until suddenly, from the crest of the old lateral moraine, the wasting trunk of the Hooker Glacier stretches out below. The death of the glacier is prolonged by a shroud of stones which shield the old ice from the sun's glare. But the rattle of stones and widening circles in the blue melt lake mark the inevitable shrinking of a glacier that was once a wide and white highway between the ranges. On the eastern side of the glacier perfectly sculpted terraces mark the high tide marks of advances in past times and it is hard to believe that only eighty years ago the surface of the Hooker Glacier was perhaps eighty metres higher than now and clear ice extended some kilometres below its present terminal above the Hooker Hut.

There are gullies to cross and a climb through scrub to the highest moraine terrace; buttercups thin slowly as altitude increases, scree gullies shimmer in the heat across the valley, waterfalls drain tortured ice in hanging basins far above. Southward the rocky Sealy Range rises above the discreet blue roofs of the Hermitage hotel complex; north, beyond the sliding curve of scree—always Mount Cook. Sunset or sunrise colours the high ice, seen from the convivial door of Hooker Hut; primus roar, buffet of early morning wind; keas come to share supper or breakfast and a swirling river of fine weather fog burgeons up the valley to cool the dawn climb.

There are orange marker posts and cairns, maybe buried by snow early in the season. Up from the hut, over gullies, then the steep spur; shattered rock and snowpatch; steep bluff; deepening gullies on either hand with blistered ice. Fitzgerald Pass to the left looks easy and enticing but—stick to the spur, delicate foothold here, a pull there, rest, bending over your ice axe, hitch up the pack and stare at Cook between your legs. The going is mostly easy, sometimes hard, always steep, demanding care and fitness; but elevation is swift and in a few hours the worst is over. Ahead, on the top of the spur, the silver, barrel-like emergency shelter defies the wind, a haven for those caught out by a turn in the weather or over-estimation of their ability and fitness.

Beyond, the final snow and ice, a crevasse that must be turned with care and the rocky notches of the pass. Now, in the southern view, there is the Tasman Valley, Lake Pukaki and the Mackenzie Country; the configuration of Mount Cook is clearer with the appearance of the west face, the High Peak and the summit ridge, the 'roof of New Zealand'. Mount Dampier, third highest, is dwarfed at Cook's flank and Hicks closes the head of the Hooker Valley.

The pass may be crossed at a number of points, better to the south, and always early, before the cloud builds up from Westland and spills over the Main Divide, even on a fine day. Cloud can cause anxiety, danger of losing the way, apart from the aesthetic disadvantage of losing the view. The most favoured travellers may see out to the Tasman Sea at the mouth of the Karangarua River. More likely, cloud will hang heavy in the lower valleys, glooming bush and gorge; the Copland Valley will seem impossibly far below, the river unmoving, tall rimu and totara part of the tight curls fastened to the hillsides; hot pools unimaginable in one's surroundings of snow, keen wind and vaulting peaks. A final look east—to bare rock, ice and the distant hot yellow of dry tussocks; then down to the west, to forest and river where a traveller might be more at ease.

In the first gully down from the pass the wind may be cold and unpleasant; but quickly the slope merges into easy basins, snow and scree, dropping from level to level in the dramatic loss of height and consequent changes in vegetation and landform which are the outstanding features of the Copland Track. In the lower basin the marked track appears again after the snowy wastes of the pass region, meandering through tussocks and rocks beside the deep creek and gorged waterfall. There are snow buttercups, then mountain buttercups, then, as one descends the zigzag into the valley head, plants thicken and vary in a vast subalpine garden that stretches for kilometres down valley to the bushline at the first big bend of the river. This great band of scrub and shrubs is broken only by three shingle gullies which carry drainage from the cliffs of the Main Divide, or avalanching snow in spring. Foxglove and snowgrass, wild carrot and fuschia, ribbonwood and snow totara, flax and toetoe, spaniard and daisy.

The track is defined and graded again, perhaps hidden by the profusion of plants. There is a feeling of gathering confinement as height is lost and the valley bluffs close in. For the first time since leaving the lower Hooker Valley a river's roar becomes steady company, distinct from alpine silences that were broken only by the rush of wind, the rumble of avalanche and the shriek of keas. The keas are gone, and soaring gull; pipits belong to the scrub and tussock, and furtive, stalking wekas. After a day of steep climbing and long, unending descent, in wind or under sun reflected from rock and snow, there is sudden protection, coolness, dimming light, the smell of trees and moist earth. One moment there is scree and messy scrub, next the forest and, in a few moments, the hidden shelter of Douglas Rock Hut.

Those with time and energy will do well to persevere for another two hours or so, losing still more height along the undulating bush path with frequent glimpses of the bouldered river. For the great descent is only complete at the flats which are no less welcome than when Charlie Douglas first broke on to them from the west. Seventeen hundred metres it has been, down from the pass, to the level of grass and stones, guarded by the sawtooth Sierras on the south. Now a final jogging walk to the end of Welcome Flat, marked by the evening calls of long-tailed cuckoos and paradise ducks—to the bridge at the start of the gorge, fantastic striated rocks in the water below. Beyond lies the hut, chimney smoke mixing with mist and the sulphurous steam of the mineral pools. What better than an hour's soak, submerged below sandfly level, adjusting the flow of hot water to suit one's tired limbs, looking up at the bush, enormous bluffs, happy at cooling rain and the innumerable waterfalls it brings?

Eighteen kilometres to go, nearly all through bush, a respite and contrast to the previous days. The track is clear and benched and easy to follow so that there is time to study the forest and its life—massive rimu and totara, lancewood and kamahi, flaming rata if you travel at New Year. Red flowers or white set against the misty river or dark bluffs. Pigeons plump and noisily whooshing beneath the tree canopies, searching for berries; bellbird, tomtit, flocks of waxeyes.

At first the track stays high above the river where it ploughs through semi-gorge, but it drops steadily 300 more metres to Architect Creek. Beyond the creek bridge it meets river boulders, then moves back to the bush and then back to the river again where huge rocks in midstream are worn to incredible shapes. In heavy rain Architect Creek may become bank-to-bank flood and the Copland River may rise perceptibly in minutes. The smallest creeks become dangerous crossings and though footbridges at Shiels and Palaver creeks may look incongruous in fine weather, they are lifesavers in the wet.

The longest stretch of Copland boulders leads to a short climb and a straight and wide bush highway. There is a strange silence as the river is left behind and one walks along the bridle track that took oldtimers by horse all the way to the Cook River. Though eroded now, it provides an easy path for tired legs on the several kilometres that remain to the track's end. A brief side excursion allows one to look out over the junction of the Copland River with its superior, the Karangarua. Then it is not far to the flats, the cabbage trees, the fern trees, perhaps sheep or cattle and that signpost that seems to get no nearer—the Karangarua suspension bridge.

The tramp over the final flats provides time to reflect on a journey of incomparable contrasts. In the mind's eye Mount Cook may be framed by fern and flowering rata, ice by buttercup and flax. The Copland Track provides almost the total experience of Southern Alps landscape. Perhaps one day is will be complete when the track goes on, beyond the severing motor road, through more flats, bush and swamp to the thunder of Tasman surf—ocean to the west, towering peaks to the east.

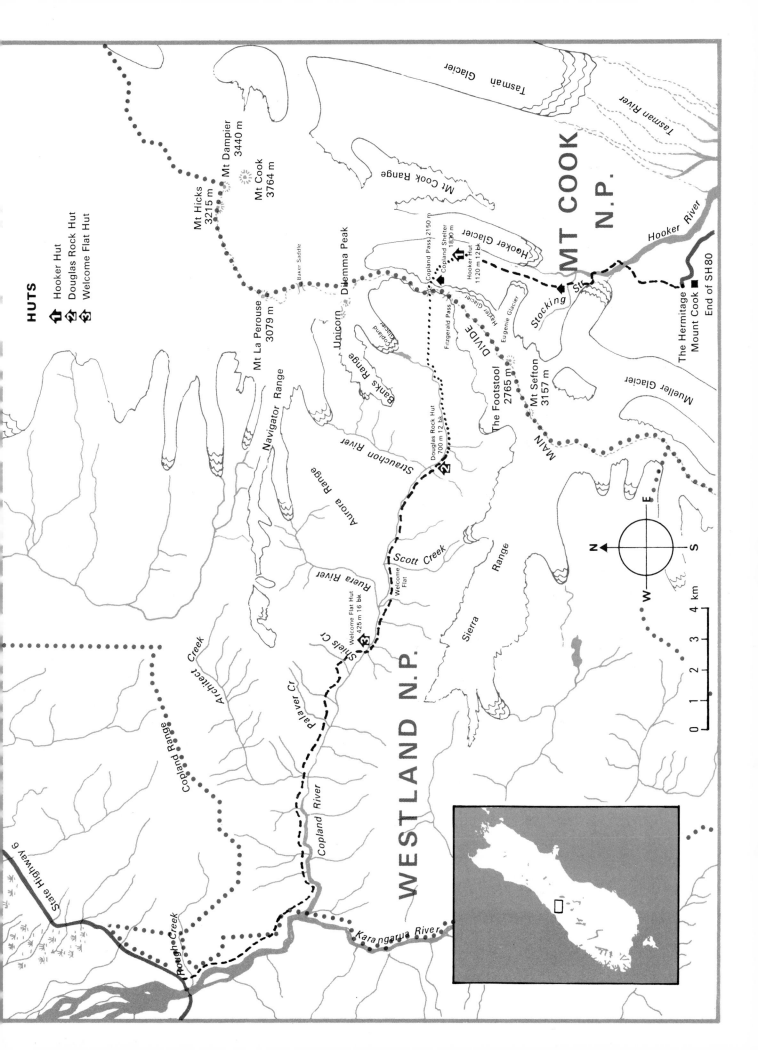

Copland Valley from the pass; Mount Sefton
and the Footstool upper left

Horrid Spaniard, *Aciphylla horrida*

Giant buttercups, *Ranunculus lyallii*

Feathery leaved buttercup,
Ranunculus seriocophyllus

Large mountain daisy,
Celmisia coriacea

Architect Creek in flood

South face of Mount Cook from the pass

Sierra Range from Welcome Flat

Rata in the lower Copland

REES-DART

FALCON

89

Spaniard, *Aciphylla* sp.

Rees Saddle at sunset

Silver beech leaves

Dart River from Sandy Bluff

Source of
the Rees
River

THE FOUR tracks described so far are separated both by distance and sharply differing character: the mysterious bush country of Waikaremoana; the stark volcanic highlands of Tongariro; the hills, basins and nikau coast of the Heaphy; the high alpine country of the Copland. The remaining four tracks are contiguous; it is almost possible to step from one to another. This might suggest a sameness, a repetition in landscape and natural qualities. Yet in this region the Southern Alps, the eastern lake country, the granite humps of Fiordland, and South Westland river forest all meet in a geographic jigsaw that provides a final picture of contrasting landscape unmatched anywhere else in New Zealand.

First, the Rees-Dart Valley system, the epitome of the beech forest-big river scene on the eastern slopes of the Southern Alps. Snow and ice flanked peaks rise to over 2700 metres on either hand as one walks over the tussock flats beside the Rees River or through the dense forest beside the long-running Dart; emerging from trees to secluded flats or tenuous bluff ledges that look out to the trackless mountain ridges of the Barrier Range. Then the Routeburn, which drains into the lower Dart and offers a varied path across the end of the Southern Alps Main Divide; a bridge from alpine beech forest to the long, low Hollyford River whose valley reaches through rimu and rata to the sea at Martins Bay. Beyond both are the sudden grey walls of Fiordland and the incomparable canyon trail of the Milford. To those with both the time and energy, the consecutive walking of these tracks provides the opportunity for a close appreciation of the varied natural forces and influences that have created the bush and mountain country of the South Island.

The Rees and Dart rivers both drain into the head of Lake Wakatipu, running down old glacial valleys either side of the Forbes Mountains, effectively separating this range from the Southern Alps Divide (the Barrier Range) to the north and the dry Richardson Mountains to the east. The Forbes peaks are like the summits of an island where Mount Earnslaw reaches 2819 metres above its glaciers. With Aspiring to the north and Tutoko to the south, it forms a triumvirate of great peaks south of the Mount Cook region. The work of glaciers in shaping the landscape can be seen in the depth of the valleys and their high steep shoulders topped by the cirques of hanging glaciers long disappeared or still alive and active beneath the summits of the Forbes and Barrier ranges. Then the rivers came to carve through the glacial deposits of rock and dust, forming pleasant elevated terraces and braided skeins of water and shingle.

Vegetation grew according to climate: wetter and colder to the north and west where the Dart Valley lies in the shadow of the Main Divide; drier and warmer in the Rees, which is partially sheltered from the prevailing westerlies by the Forbes Mountains. The forest is beech. Red beech dominates the moist but warmer regions of the lower Dart, but finds the Rees too dry. Silver beech fills the upper reaches of the Dart. But the Rees displays almost pure mountain beech, the most drought-resistant of the three species, filling even gullies of the barren Richardson Mountains.

In considering form and vegetation and climate, the Rees contrasts sharply with the Dart: open flats and valley head with bush-choked gorge and looming ice. The high peaks seem to lie back from the floor of the Rees, a distant serrated skyline dominated by the smooth cone of Earnslaw. In the Dart the mountains press close; snowfield and turret, ice above vertiginous bluff. Together the valleys allow a varied walk through mountains and beside glaciers, where the traveller need climb no higher than 1500 metres in crossing the pass that joins the heads of the two rivers.

The Maoris knew the lower reaches of both valleys, but the upper reaches were unknown until Europeans came looking for gold. The attentions of most early prospectors and explorers were centered on the Routeburn region of the lower Dart (see next track) and the Rees Valley. In 1861 W. G. Rees of Queenstown established a sheep station near the present site of Glenorchy and the following year the first prospectors sailed up the lake and began searching for colour in the big rivers and their tributaries. When young surveyor James McKerrow arrived in February 1863 he found 'the atmosphere so loaded with smoke from the fires lighted by diggers that the prospect was obscured in every direction'. McKerrow travelled up the Rees to about the confluence of Hunter Stream and described the valley as 'very well grassed' and having 'upwards of 10,000 acres of prime agricultural or pastoral land'. He met prospectors everywhere, 'confining their attentions to the gullies that open into the main valley where they expected a better result'.

The first journey to the head of the Rees and beyond was made the following year. Explorer and prospector Patrick Caples crossed Rees Saddle with five miners and looked for gold down the Snowy Creek to the Dart but results were poor and the party soon gave up. He came back to describe the source of the Dart River—'a very large glacier, surrounded by perpendicular mountains'. After this abortive foray, diggers showed little interest in the upper Rees, but there were lucrative finds in the lower valley, near the start of the present walking track. Small-scale mining continued through the 1860s and 1870s, but in 1882 the Invincible Company set up a quartz battery on the creek of the same name and continued operations until the turn of the century. Relics in the valley and on the hillside bear witness to the area's mining heyday.

In the 1870s the Rees was taken up as a sheep run, the Rees Valley Station occupying all the flats and terraces on the wide eastern bank, with stock being run beyond the upper gorge into the open basins at the head of the river. The only man-made shelters in the valley are station musterers' huts at Arthur Creek, Twenty-five Mile Creek (built in 1897 and later given to the Otago Tramping Club) and Shelter Rock near the bushline. (A new national park hut is planned for this site.)

Mountaineering began with Irishman Rev. W. S. Green and his party who travelled south to tackle Mount Earnslaw after their unsuccessful attempt on Mount Cook in March 1882. They found no better luck in the south, for the snow and wind of a nor'wester overcame them barely half way up the mountain. Writing of the climb, he described how 'Immediately at our feet the ridge fell away in precipices to the Rees river, which all but monopolized the narrow bottom of the deep defile over 2000 feet below us; the only signs of human life being at one spot where some men had conducted a watercourse along the opposite hill-side, towards a gold-working in a quartz reef. . . .' But Green had a low opinion of the diggers and thought the settlement of industrious Swiss settlers in beech chalets a much better prospect for the future. 'Let them build their homes and cultivate their little patches of ground, and then there will be a healthier life in these glens than gold-grubbing can ever bring.'

The mountaineering and scenic attractions of the Mount Earnslaw region generated a strong local tourist industry. Accommodation, guiding and transport services in 1889 were a good deal more varied than today. As a base for climbing or walking in the area, one could bed down at the Alpine Club, Glenorchy or Mount Earnslaw hotels at Glenorchy or the Glacier Hotel at Kinloch. Excursions were advertised up the Rees as far as Lennox Falls— by buggy and horse; and climbs of Mount Bonpland and to within 200 metres of the summit of Earnslaw, whose summit was still inviolate. Testimonials described the accommodation as excellent, the horses capital and chief guide Harry Birley as first rate. Birley made the first ascent of Earnslaw, alone, in 1890.

Climbing expeditions completed exploration of both valleys and their surrounding mountains and were particularly important in opening up the middle and upper reaches of the Dart. The lower Dart as far as Chinamans Bluff was early explored and used for sheepfarming. But, as the name of the bluff suggests, Chinese goldminers were the first to live and work in the middle valley as far as Cattle Flat, named later for the practice of cattle grazing which continues to this point even today. In 1900 a gold dredge was built at Dredge Flat. All materials for the dredge operation (except timber) had to be hauled by wagon all the way from Glenorchy wharf, including a complete sawmilling plant. Despite this superhuman effort, dredging was not a success and the site was abandoned after a year. The dilapidated company hut remains to provide shelter in the middle valley and bits of the old dredge may still be seen, buried in the nearby river beach.

Explorations by surveyors and geologists were focussed on the valleys and peaks of the Humboldt Mountains and the Olivines. Until the turn of the century, the upper Dart was largely unknown and had been visited only once, by Caples's party in 1864. Another prospector made the first crossing of the Barrier Range in 1897, from Cattle Flat in the Dart to the Joe River tributary of the Arawata River. This was William O'Leary, the legendary Arawata Bill. But, as West Coast explorer Charlie Douglas noted, he kept information about the area to himself.

The upper Dart was finally explored in the years immediately before World War I by Major Bernard Head's parties. In 1911 he crossed from the West Matukituki Valley and travelled down the Dart to Paradise with Mount Cook guides Jack Clarke and J. P. Murphy. In 1914 he led a major expedition which established a base camp on Cattle Flat and, striking out from there, surveyed the Dart Glacier and made several first ascents of peaks in the upper valley. The exploration of the region's peaks and passes, glaciers and alpine basins was not completed until Jack Holloway unravelled the mysteries of the Barrier Range in the 1930s.

Tramping tracks in both valleys were completed by the start of World War II and the round trip became an increasingly popular excursion after 1945. Most of the tracks were cut by prospectors and runholders and were open by the turn of the century; but the upper Dart beyond Cattle Flat was virtually virgin bush until the mid-1930s. Men on government relief work during the Depression cut a horse track towards the junction of the Dart and the Snowy and contract workers completed the final five kilometres to Dart Hut in 1939. The hut was built for the New Zealand Alpine Club in 1937, single-handed by mountain guide Kurt Suter. Materials for the hut were carried by packhorse from Paradise to the end of the incomplete track and then back-packed through the bush to the building site. Still comfortable and solid after forty years, it is a monument to one man's gruelling labour and skill.

Since 1964 the Dart region has been part of Mount Aspiring National Park, so that tracks and bridges in the valley are maintained to a high standard. Although the western side of the Rees is also in national park, the Rees section of the track crosses the property of the Rees Valley Station as far as the head of the valley. The track is clear and generally well marked but is more tenuous in the alpine basins below Rees Saddle. Vehicular access at both ends of the track has been slowly extended. At present four-wheel-drive vehicles can reach Chinamans Bluff in the Dart and Twenty-five Mile Hut in the Rees. In dry weather ordinary cars can be taken safely to near the old mine site at Invincible Creek in the Rees—the usual starting point for trampers—and a good road may eventually reach Chinamans Bluff too. Fortunately, gorge and bluff and national park protection will prevent any further road encroachments.

∞∞∞

One can start the round trip in either the Dart or the Rees. But the easy, open nature of the lower Rees, and the valley's gradual climb to the highest point of the trip at Rees Saddle, encourage most people to begin here. The lower part of the Rees may prove disappointing to many, for the walk is mostly along a wide vehicle track, in places cut with little regard for hill form and forest. But between McDougalls Creek and Bridges Creek there are the compensations of close mountain beech tumbling steeply down to the bouldery river which is at the height of its power as it forces a way through the narrow valley. Snow mountains are glimpsed through the trees and a pause for rest in the bush is likely to attract the attention of the almost silent but tame grey robin.

Beyond Bridges Creek, rolling eight kilometres to the junction of Hunter Stream, are wide yellow flats, airy and warm on a clear day, tussock against the legs, sun glaring off glaciers on the Forbes Mountains. Swinging easily over the flats towards Twenty-five Mile Hut, the summit of Earnslaw comes steadily into view, 2300 metres above. Across the river, water from the glacier beneath the peak thrashes down in Lennox Falls, once the focus of Harry Birley's tourist excursions. Above, at the bushline, is Kea Basin and its hut, a traditional base for climbers. Sheep range over the flats and the open spurs of the Richardson Mountains to the east, and birds of the open country and riverbed are common—oystercatchers, paradise ducks, hawks and even the spur-winged plover.

The real delights of the Rees begin as the flats dwindle and the forest closes in once more near where the river must be forded above the Hunter Stream junction. Here the final traces of vehicle tracks are left behind and over the river the track rises and falls through the beech forest, leaves shimmering as sunlight glances through the canopy of trees and small breezes rise from the gorged river. The margin of the river is reached again in secluded grassy clearings; and at the Clarke Slip the valley seems to expand where lichen-coloured cairns show the way towards the last forest and the snow-seamed buttresses of Mounts Clarke and Cunningham which fill the head of the valley. Throughout this section of the track there are innumerable idyllic camp sites among the forest clearings.

During the last hour of steady climbing from Slip Flat to Shelter Rock the forest is increasingly broken by small grassy hollows and spurs. In late afternoon there is much pleasure in moving from the coolness and shade of the forest into the warmth of sunlight slanting down the western bluffs. The tiny Shelter Rock Hut is cossetted in the last bay of beech forest; beyond lie the open subalpine slopes leading to the Rees Saddle.

The upper reaches of the Rees are perhaps the highlight of the entire trip. The track is more difficult to follow and the steady ascent is sometimes rough through scrub. But the wealth of subalpine shrubs, bushes and flowers, merging finally into the high snow tussocks, more than compensate for these discomforts. The Rees, now a mountain creek, is forded once again and from the spur above one may finally look back down the valley to the towering white cone of Earnslaw, framed in early summer by the golden heads of flowering spaniards. The basin below the Rees Saddle is a sanctuary of tussock and stream, boulder and sheltered hollow, guarded perhaps by falcons and frequented by chamois and goats. In fine summer weather there is no better place to camp, to enjoy the peace and the clear sharp grandeur of a mountain night.

The climb to the Rees Saddle is finally steep but without difficulty. Beyond, the world is wholly alpine. There is no sign of softening forest, simply tussock and rock, snow and ice, the mass of Headlong Peak and a hint of greater peaks and glaciers to come. Snowy Creek swerves down its narrow gorge, steeply down to the Dart. This section of the track—from the Rees Saddle to Dart Hut—is the most difficult and potentially dangerous. The track is well marked down to the Snowy, which is spanned by a footbridge. But the slopes are steep and slippery—more so with rain or snow—and the way from the bridge to the hut is broken, rough and indistinct. Speargrass is everywhere to jab the unwary hand or calf. Yet the toilsome, wearying descent to the hut may be alleviated as the grand peaks of the Barrier Range slowly swing into view above the broad sweep of the Whitbourn Glacier. In early summer, if one is fortunate, there may be fields of glorious giant mountain buttercups on the lower slopes.

Dart Hut, at the edge of silver beech forest, offers security and ease before the long trek down the Dart; or it may be used as a base for excursions into the alpine amphitheatre of the Dart Glacier. The journey down the Dart is usually undertaken in two stages: down to Daleys Flat and its hut, then out to the roadhead at Paradise. The stages are long—19 and 29 kilometres respectively—but the well-hewn track makes for easy and fast travelling. The forest is dominant, dense on either bank of the Dart River—longer, deeper and more powerful than the Rees. The valley widens only slowly and one is constantly aware of great bluffs, ice and high mountains on either hand.

The long stretch of forest on the first stage is broken by Cattle Flat, nearly five kilometres long and not so much a flat as a sloping open terrace above the river, broken by stream ravines; a place to camp or to rest in the heat of the day, leaning back to view the shelves of glaciers and the pass that Arawata Bill pioneered to the West Coast eighty years ago. Beyond Cattle Flat the track descends markedly and the river disappears in a distant rumble as it thunders down its gorge. River and track meet again beside the quiet reaches of Quinns and Daleys Flats (named for prospectors of the 1880s), a relief to eyes grown accustomed to a never-ending vista of dark beech trees. One may stop at the hut or push on to the crumbling shelter of Dredge Hut—renowned for its sandflies!

Below Dredge the forest is broken regularly by clearings and the river broadens, swinging back and forth, cutting into the great bluffs. The track soon climbs and clings to the face of Sandy Bluff and from a terrace blasted in the rock one may look out to the valley of the Bride Burn and the Cosmos Peaks above Lake Mystery. Beyond Sandy Bluff, great rocks called The Sisters defy the power of the river in midstream as the water swirls and smokes with spray through a narrow defile in the forest.

The final stages of the Dart track wind through forest and over flats to Chinamans Bluff. The Barrier Range peaks are left behind and the Humboldt Mountains dominate the view, with the twisted Mount Nox as a cornerstone to the valley of the Beans Burn. If one is at Chinamans in wet weather, there is shelter under Arawata Bill's old rock bivouac and if the nor'wester blows well there may be the sight across the valley of the Lake Unknown falls streaming upwards in the wind.

Now there are the final kilometres to Paradise, through paddock and bush, the scene suddenly domesticated by road and cattle and sheep. The walk has been long and memories will be dominated by forest and river close at hand, peaks and glaciers at a distance. But against the broad scene there will have been the particular delights of bird and plant life—swooping falcon or fragile buttercup. And in the sum, an extended experience of life and nature in the beech forest and subalpine world of the Southern Alps.

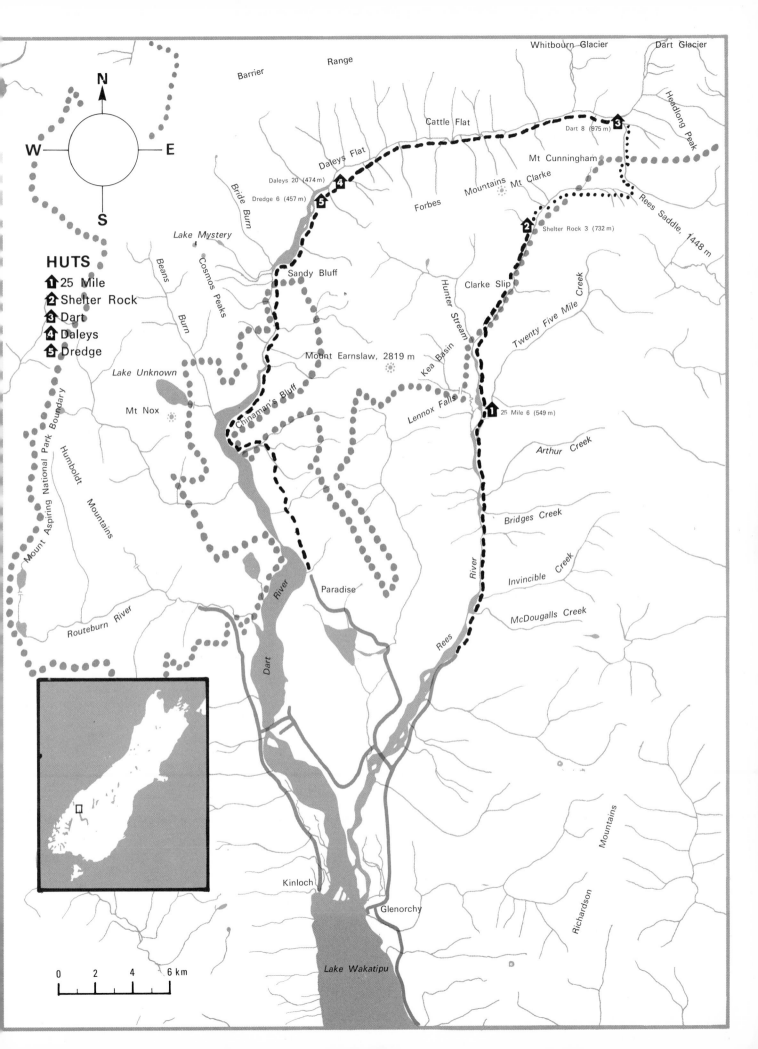

Boulders in Snowy Creek at the upper crossing

Mount
Earnslaw
from the
pper Rees

Daleys Flat, Dart Valley

Route cairn

Sunset clouds over the Barrier Range; from Dredge Flat

Moss
covered
beech,
upper
Dart

ROUTEBURN

TOMTIT

Earland Falls

Harris Saddle; Darran Mountains beyond

Mountain beech, Lake Mackenzie

Routeburn Falls

Lake
Mackenzie
Emily Pea
beyond

THE KEY to the history of this track lies in its name. To Maoris mining greenstone and to European prospectors, surveyors, scientists and mountain explorers, the valley of the Routeburn and the passes at its head formed a vital route from Lake Wakatipu to the mineral-rich ranges to the northwest, and to the great Hollyford River and its tributaries running down to the coast of South Westland. The region's historical importance derives from its geographical significance. Though the Routeburn Track stretches for less than forty kilometres, it traverses the end of the chain of the Southern Alps and looks out to the granite fastnesses of Fiordland. From Key Summit, at the western end of the track, one looks north down the deep valley of the Hollyford to Martins Bay in Westland; south to the Eglinton River, running to lakes Te Anau and Manapouri which ultimately drain through the Waiau River to the sea at Foveaux Strait; east to the Greenstone River, draining to Wakatipu and thus to the great Clutha River and the coast of Otago; west to the canyons and fiords of New Zealand's greatest national park. For the traveller, the Routeburn Track ties together the massively sculptured landforms and natural features that typify the bush and mountain heartland of the South Island.

There are traces of Maori villages near the mouth of the Routeburn; and a remarkable sequence of Maori names from Lake Wakatipu via Te Komama (Routeburn) and Tarahaka Whakatipu (Harris Saddle) to Whakatipu Waitai (Lake McKerrow-Martins Bay) reveals the importance of the route to them in working lodes of precious greenstone and for trading between villages in South Westland and Central Otago. The Routeburn as a source of greenstone remained important to the Maoris until the nineteenth century and it is said that the last Maori greenstone expedition left the east coast for the Routeburn in 1852.

Wakatipu was first seen by a European the following year and in 1861 David McKellar and George Gunn, after exploring the Greenstone Valley, climbed further to peaks near Harris Saddle and returned to describe the run of the Hollyford and the sweep of the Darran Mountains in Fiordland. 1861 saw the start of the Otago gold rushes and by 1862 the first prospectors were probing the mountains of the Rees and the Dart. Road access to the rich goldfields of the Queenstown-Arrowtown region was initially very difficult from Dunedin, which lay more than 300 kilometres away on the east coast. It was rumoured that there was an easy route to the west coast through the mountains northwest of Wakatipu—perhaps only eighty kilometres long. If a pass was found, a port could be established that would allow fast trading links with the cities of Australia.

In 1862 and 1863 prospectors explored the Routeburn. First North Col was reached, but not crossed. Then P. Q. Caples—who first crossed Rees Saddle in 1864—discovered Harris Saddle and made a solo journey down the Hollyford (both of which he named). But none of Caples's information reached James Hector, the young and zealous chief geologist to the Provincial Government of Otago. Determined to prove a good road route from Wakatipu to Martins Bay, he first explored the way up the Greenstone Valley from the lake, then he sailed to the West Coast, travelled up the Hollyford, connecting the two valleys and arrived in Queenstown in October 1863 to a tumultuous welcome by miners who already visualised bullion-laden coaches making daily journeys to a thriving port at Martins Bay. But the business community of Dunedin had already sensed the danger and prevailed upon Provincial Government to quickly complete coach roads to the east. A road to the west would mean Otago gold in Australian banks across the Tasman, and a trade pattern that would favour the towns of Victoria and New South Wales and not Dunedin. Business was business.

Prospectors continued to use the Routeburn as a way to dreamed-of wealth in the unknown ranges to the north. The most spectacular prospecting journeys in New Zealand's history were undertaken by Alphonse Barrington and his companions between December 1863 and June 1864. Using the North Col, they explored vast tracts of unknown mountain country at the headwaters of the Hollyford, Pyke and Cascade rivers. They made a dugout canoe to cross Lake Alabaster, tackled snow and glaciers in efforts to find mountain passes to the Dart. In the roughest country they had ever encountered, accident nearly claimed each member of the party. Barrington wrote: 'Simonin was behind me, I heard him sing out "Look out!" I turned round and he was coming down the snow at a fearful rate, head first, on his back.' Simonin came to rest at the bottom of a gully and 'I thought he was killed, but he was all right, with the exception of being a little frightened.' Another man—Farrell—survived amazingly when a flax rope broke and he fell into a powerful cataract but saved himself by clinging to a rock. The party nearly perished from starvation. As they struggled back to Wakatipu down the Routeburn, Barrington wrote in his diary: 'If fasting and praying is of any value to sinners, we ought to become saints, for we have had enough of it lately.' It is recorded that when the men returned to Queenstown they were taken to hospital, given £40 by friendly miners and a public meeting voted its thanks for their exploratory work. But Barrington had found few traces of gold to stimulate a rush and already news of rich finds on the West Coast near Hokitika were claiming attention.

In 1870 plans for a road to Martins Bay were resurrected with the proposal to establish a farming settlement there. Surveyor James McKerrow examined the Routeburn and Harris Saddle and declared that a bridle track could be cut through for £400. But he was optimistic and work on the bridle track was abandoned in the lower Routeburn after four years' effort. A good pack track was completed as far as Harris Saddle and for two years mail was carried by contract all the way to the bay. But the settlement languished and the Hollyford track fell into disrepair. Over the subsequent hundred years there has been steady development of the Routeburn section of the track as an attraction for tourists and trampers. In this role it pre-dates the Milford Track by fifteen years.

Harry Bryant of Kinloch and Harry Birley of Glenorchy took tourists up to Harris Saddle in the 1880s and 1890s. Mounted parties of up to seventeen rode to a night camp on the Routeburn Flats, then the following morning climbed on foot to the Saddle for the view, returning to Kinloch on the same day. When the Milford Track was a going concern much more ambitious treks were undertaken that would daunt all but the hardened tramper today. By horse to the Routeburn Flats; on foot over the Harris Saddle; down to the Hollyford; up to Lake Howden at the head of the Greenstone; along the Livingstone Range; down into the Eglinton Valley at Cascade Creek; over the Dore Pass to the Milford Track; a return journey to Milford Sound, ending at Lake Te Anau—a good two-and-a-half-week summer holiday!

An enthusiastic Minister of Tourism, Sir Thomas Mackenzie, initiated the high-level extension of the track from Harris Saddle to Lake Howden in 1912. Harry Birley investigated the route and discovered Lake Mackenzie. Construction began a year later and by the outbreak of war was complete except for the zigzag above the lake. Supplies for the track workers were carried up from Kinloch by Thomas Bryant, who persuaded horses to tackle the bogs of the upper Routeburn basins and the rocky approaches to the Saddle. On one trip a packhorse became jammed with its load against a bluff. The more prosaic story has it that Bryant was forced to entirely unload the horse and then reload it once he had moved it past the obstacle; colourful myth relates that Bryant did nothing until the work gang arrived and dynamited away the offending rock.

The Bryant family of Kinloch has been associated with the Routeburn Track since its inception. First Harry, then Thomas, guided tourists up the Routeburn and beyond as the track was extended. The younger Harry followed the family tradition and in 1929 began a motor service along the road from Kinloch into the Routeburn. The Bryant connection with Routeburn tourism did not cease until 1974 when the bridge across the lower Dart made the Routeburn accessible to private motorists.

The improvement of roads and the building of the Dart bridge has taken some of the romance away from the Routeburn, a romance generated by its inaccessibility and remoteness beyond the lake, hidden among high mountains. Until the early 1930s walking the Routeburn meant a return journey down the Greenstone Valley, back to Wakatipu. In 1929 the road towards Milford Sound went no further than the township of Te Anau; but relief workers during the Depression built the road up the Eglinton Valley to the start of the Homer Tunnel. Just before World War II the final section of the Routeburn Track was cut—from Lake Howden, around Key Summit to the Milford road.

Access to the eastern end of the track was by water until early 1974. There was excitement and pleasure in boarding the stately lake steamer *Earnslaw* for a three-hour cruise up the lake, calling with mail and supplies at Walter Peak and Mount Nicholas stations along the way. Then there was the humour and colour of Harry Bryant's commentary as his open air bus lumbered slowly over the twenty kilometres of rough road to the start of the track. By 1970 the *Earnslaw* had been withdrawn from this service. The Queenstown-Glenorchy road had been opened in 1962 and was improved so that buses could take over. The Bryant launch trip from Glenorchy to Kinloch was finally replaced by the Dart road bridge in 1974. This might not be the end of the encroachment of the motorcar. A costly bridge demands use. Firm plans show a road south of Kinloch, then up the Greenstone—the traditional track—to join the Milford road by Key Summit. The end of the Routeburn Track will be severed. Though the track lies wholly within national parks (Aspiring from the mouth of the Routeburn to Harris Saddle; Fiordland from the Saddle to Key Summit), the parks themselves seem to be no defence against the demands of commercial operators, the needs of the package bus tour. One can rest more easily in the knowledge that the remainder of the Routeburn Track is unlikely to be violated because, as James McKerrow discovered back in 1870, the country is too difficult for a road.

The track may be walked from either end, but there is a sense of exploration in starting from the mouth of the Routeburn Valley, following in the footsteps of Caples, Barrington and those other early explorers who pushed into the unknown from the valley's head.

At the end of the access road one is already hemmed about by beech forest and close mountains. There is little suggestion of the wide valley of the Dart to the east, or the bare tussock hills cradling Wakatipu, the South Island's second largest lake. And at first there seems no way to the west, no passage through the abrupt walls, rock bluffs laced by waterfalls, and bush-filled gorge. But the wide benched track on the north bank of the Routeburn climbs and sidles easily through the trees, entering the gorge high above the river, making a way to the flats of the upper valley with surprising ease—a tribute to the skill and work of the pioneering track cutters.

At first the track follows the edge of the river but soon it begins a graded climb, canopied by forest. Contrast to the unending vista of climbing trees is afforded by the cascading break of cold streams. Early on, the character of the track surface changes and looking back one can see the last stretch of the 1870s road, crumbled at the sides and edged by young trees. Birds may be scarce or plentiful, depending on the season; there may be parakeets, a robin to sit on your boot and always fantails at the edge of the water.

The enclosing stillness of the forest is broken in the gorge with the pounding of the river through massive boulders jammed beneath the trees. The track maintains its height but as the bed of the river rises, the rushing green water draws closer and one can descend to the edge of the sculptured rocks, study patterns of moss and perhaps dream a little of Maori travellers picking their way through the moist, sunless defile.

Distances on the Routeburn are not great and a couple of hours after leaving the road one will emerge from the gorge and forest on to the upper tussock flats. The flats were the old limit to horse traffic and, at the far end, bluffs whitened by the Routeburn Falls seem to bar the way. But the track takes to the forest again and, still benched and wide, it climbs easily on the southern slopes of the valley to emerge at the crest of the falls on bushline after another hour's travel. From the huts one can look back down to the flats and gorge. Beyond the steep spurs which hide the beginning of the track rise the black ramparts of Turret Head on the Earnslaw range and a wide gulf indicates the valley of the Dart. In a few hours road, valley, bush and gorge have been travelled and left behind in climbing 500 metres to a subalpine world at the tail of the Southern Alps Main Divide. The 'hut keas' will probably greet you, or wake you in the morning by sliding down the hut roof, and cause expletives to be added to the vocabulary of superlatives which have been mostly in use to that point in exclaiming on the scenery. Below lies a confined world of forest; above, the open and airy world of boulder and tussock basins, edged by rock ridges that are outlined by snow in spring and autumn.

The climbing continues, a final 300 metres, another hour or two, to the gateway of Harris Saddle. The track becomes boggy, though still well defined, rising across the southern side of the basin. The Scottish flavour of the Routeburn's name seems more appropriate now to the clear stony creek that runs through the tussocks before it makes its final leap into the forest through the falls. In early summer one might chance on beds of subalpine flowers, but here, as in so many other regions of the Southern Alps, the plant life has been reduced and damaged by the grazing of deer and chamois. But subalpine flowers are not showy—save for the giant buttercup and flowering spaniard—and a careful scrutiny beside streams or in the shelter of boulders will reveal daisy and gentian, ourisia and coprosma beneath the overhanging wave of tussock.

Higher up, one's attention is held by waterfall and grey rock and the dip of ridges towards the Saddle. The track seems to climb too high and suddenly Lake Harris comes into view, seemingly dammed in its small high basin, colour changing with sun or cloud. It may seem grim in rain, icy and repellent if snow blankets the steep mountain walls; but a source of glittering refreshment on a hot summer's day. The track edges above it, hewn and blasted from the rock. One is so occupied with the sight of the lake below and the distant views back over the Routeburn to the Richardson Mountains, that Harris Saddle seems to open suddenly. In a moment the world has changed. The wind skirls through; beyond are the parting mists of Fiordland, the huge space of the Hollyford Valley and the rearing barrier of the Darran Mountains; glacier, hanging valley and sharp-edged peak stretching from Christina in the south to Tutoko, chief of Fiordland, in the north. In summer this is a place to linger; but the bright orange triangle of the shelter hut reminds that storm in high places can bring tragedy to the unprepared.

From the Saddle the track remains above the bushline, roughly down a gully then awkwardly at times above the bush of the upper Hollyford. The Darran Mountains constantly catch the eye but now one can see right down the Hollyford to Lake McKerrow and the sea at Martins Bay—a great divide between the Southern Alps and Fiordland. At the head of the Hollyford, Key Summit stands clear, and one walks aloof above the dusty line of the road in the valley floor.

The Hollyford face is exposed to northwest rain and southerly cold but after a few kilometres the track turns a point and zigzags down, down 300 metres to Lake Mackenzie and huts in a tussock bay sheltered by the forest. The first trees are draped with skeins of moss, witness to heavy rains, and boulders litter the forest to the lake's edge. On a still evening or in early morning there is little to compare with the picture comprising the reality and reflection of Emily Peak and her sister. If one has a day to spare on the track, it could not be spent more profitably than in exploration of the bush and mountain margins of Lake Mackenzie.

Now the journey is upward again, regaining through mixed forest much of the height lost in the descending zigzag. The track filters through the edge of the trees, more varied now that the beech regions of the east have been left behind for the podocarps of the west. In summer the dull evergreen is broken by the rich red of rata blossom and birdlife increases with the greater variety of fruit and flower. At the summit of the climb the track brushes hard against the mountain bluffs and emerges at the foot of Earland Falls. Spray fills the air and the falls' performance on a rain-filled day will be compensation for the drenching discomfort of dripping bush.

Then down again, creek, forest and views of the Darrans until a sudden opening of the trees reveals Lake Howden, source of the Greenstone River and another way to Lake Wakatipu. From the lake's hut a final short climb leads to the side of Key Summit and the last hour's descent. A worthwhile side excursion leads up through the bush to the open tops of Key

Summit, a unique chock-stone in the geological structure of the region, a viewpoint to reveal the parting of watersheds where rivers in the valleys below run north, south and east. It is a botanist's mecca. Stunted beech trees take the place of subalpine scrub and merge into perhaps the finest bog and swamp region of our mountain lands, with plant life ranging from sundews, bladderworts and orchids to the bog forstera, bog daisy and bog pine.

In descending the final 400 metres from Key Summit to the Milford Road at The Divide, one is slowly immersed in thickening forest, closed in from the mountains and wide views that characterise much of the track. The high, quiet spacious world of the Routeburn is finally sealed off and insulated from the noisy dusty tourist road below. Thumbing a lift or waiting for the bus, one is filled with that special feeling of calm and satisfaction that only recreation in such a region of mountain, forest and lake can bring.

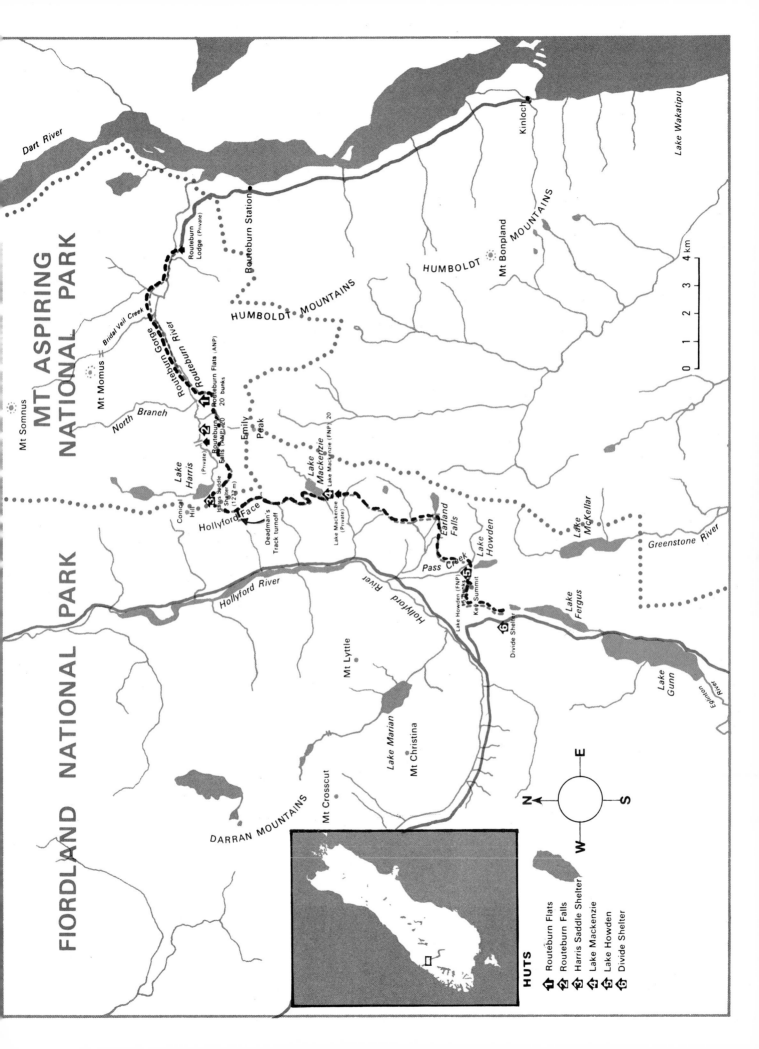

FIORDLAND NATIONAL PARK

MT ASPIRING NATIONAL PARK

Dart River

Kinloch

Lake Wakatipu

Routeburn Lodge (Private)

Routeburn Station

Mt Bonpland

HUMBOLDT MOUNTAINS

HUMBOLDT MOUNTAINS

Bridal Veil Creek

Routeburn Gorge

Routeburn River

Mt Momus

Mt Somnus

North Branch

Routeburn Flats (ANP) 20 bunks

Routeburn Falls (ANP) 20 (Private)

Emily Peak

Lake Harris

Conical Hill

Harris Saddle Shelter (1277 m)

Hollyford Face

Deadman's Track turnoff

Lake Mackenzie (FNP) 20

Lake Mackenzie

Lake Mackenzie (Private)

Earland Falls

Pass Creek

Lake Howden

Hollyford River

Hollyford River

Hollyford River

Lake Howden (FNP)

Key Summit

Divide Shelter

Lake McKellar

Greenstone River

Lake Fergus

Lake Gunn

Eglinton River

Mt Lyttle

Lake Marian

Mt Christina

Mt Crosscut

DARRAN MOUNTAINS

N
W — E
S

4 km
0 1 2 3

HUTS
1 Routeburn Flats
2 Routeburn Falls
3 Harris Saddle Shelter
4 Lake Mackenzie
5 Lake Howden
6 Divide Shelter

Routeburn Flats and gorge from edge of Routeburn Falls

122

Mount Christin
from Key Summ

Lake Harris

Ferns between Lake Mackenzie and Lake Howden

Routeburn Gorge

127

HOLLYFORD

KAKA

Hollyford River at Swamp Creek

Flax in flower (*Phormium tenax*)

River patterns, upper Hollyford

Hollyford Valley, Lake McKerrow and Martins Bay
from near Harris Saddle; Darran Mountains at left

Mount
Tutoko
from the
Lower P
Clearing

THE ENERGETIC tramper might not finish the Routeburn Track via Key Summit. Instead he may turn north at Lake Howden, descend the steep trail by Pass Creek to emerge on the Lower Hollyford road. A hitched ride there and, within an hour or two of leaving the Routeburn, he can start the 55-kilometre walk to the sea. There could be no greater natural contrast than that between the country traversed by the Routeburn and the Hollyford tracks. Though separated by only a few kilometres, a difference in altitude of several hundred metres means a total contrast in landform, vegetation and climate—the cool subalpine world of the Routeburn, the humid and dense lowland forest of the Hollyford. In human terms the contrast is vivid too. The Routeburn speaks of the exploits of explorers and gold hunters; but Hollyford history is marked by the stoic efforts of pioneering settlers to make a permanent home on the remotest coast in New Zealand.

Once there was extensive Maori settlement at Martins Bay, revealed by the evidence of old ovens and discarded tools and weapons behind the high sandhills. But when Europeans first arrived in the 1860s there remained only two families, notably Tutoko and his daughters, dubbed 'Sara and May'. The old man's name was given to the great ice peak that towers 2700 metres above the valley on the west; his daughters' names to the hills confining the bay. Sealers certainly plundered the colony at Long Reef well before 1860, and it is likely that the bay was named for one of these. But the shape and nature of the Hollyford were not revealed until McKellar and Gunn looked down on it from Key Summit in 1861.

Two years later the bay was explored and the valley opened up in the search for a port for the Central Otago goldfields and a road to connect the two. That wide-ranging prospector Patrick Quirk Caples was the first to reach Martins Bay from the Wakatipu district in March 1863. After travelling the length of the Hollyford alone, he sighted an encampment at the bay and in fear of 'wild Maoris' camped in the forest without a fire. Secretly he examined Martins Bay, 'washed his hands in the salt waters of the ocean', then made off back up the Hollyford, half starving, eating every 'Maori rabbit' (rat) that he could catch.

A few months later, an exploring party led by Captain Alabaster took a small ship over the bar of the Hollyford River and entered Lake McKerrow. Alabaster met the Maoris at the bay before taking a ship's boat up the Hollyford to explore the upper valley. His party climbed Key Summit and went up the Pyke River to discover the lake that now bears his name. Neither Alabaster nor Caples knew of the other's explorations, and Otago provincial geologist Dr James Hector still imagined he would be the first to venture up the Hollyford when he arrived at Martins Bay soon after Alabaster's departure. In modern times this lack of communication seems astonishing; but transport was slow, mails haphazard and those prospecting for new goldfields were in no hurry to pass on their finds. But the publicity attending Hector's arrival in Queenstown after his crossing from the Hollyford quickly dispelled any mysteries surrounding this route to the west coast (see Routeburn Track).

Enthusiasm for a Martins Bay port and a Hollyford road soon waned but prospectors travelled the region throughout the 1860s, using it as a link between Otago and Southland and Big Bay and Jackson Bay in South Westland. At one time the traffic must have been frequent, for the remains of a trade store were found on the shores of Lake McKerrow in 1870. But not all the diggers were fortunate enough to encounter an isolated store or settler's shack before their food and energy gave out. Deadman's Bluff near the road in the upper valley is witness to the final resting place of one unknown prospector's bones.

In 1868 the Otago Provincial Government determined on a settlement in the Martins Bay-Lake McKerrow region. The bar was said to be negotiable, the stands of timber magnificent and the rocks to promise gold and other minerals. Official enthusiasm could not be stopped, despite the tenor of a public meeting in 1870 when only eighteen of the seventy in attendance voted in favour of the settlement. One perspicacious surveyor foresaw that permanent and reliable means of communication were essential to the settlement's survival, either a road from Wakatipu or a securely engineered entrance across the Hollyford bar. But the settlement went ahead, despite provincial surveyor James McKerrow's failure to find a suitable road route and the continuing trouble that small ships had in safely entering the Hollyford River.

Town sections were surveyed at Jamestown on a bay at the northeastern corner of the lake; rural blocks on either side of the river towards the sea. Much of the land was sold but not all the buyers made the sea journey to establish their new homes. By the end of 1870 there were seven or eight houses at Jamestown; the settlement was beginning to grow. But as the years passed it became clear that no road would ever come down the Hollyford and a series of mishaps underlined the dangers of the river entrance. The settlement suffered a serious early setback when a ship carrying sawmilling machinery was totally wrecked on the bar. Transport soon depended entirely on steamers that came every two or three months and stood offshore while passengers and supplies were ferried by small boat. If the weather was rough and the surf high when the steamer arrived at Martins Bay, it simply sailed away, to return after another three months.

The terrible privations suffered by the settlers at Jamestown were simply but vividly recorded by Alice McKenzie (*Pioneers of Martins Bay*, 1947 and 1970), who arrived at the settlement with her parents in 1876. There was near starvation when the steamer failed to land provisions. 'Mrs Robertson told me how she used to gather carageen, a seaweed. . . . She boiled it in milk to make a jelly for the youngest children.' The settlers had milking cows and if 'a bullock was killed there was fresh meat for a week, and the rest had to be salted into casks'. But for much of their meat they relied on native birds and fish.

Tragedy punctuated life at Jamestown with monotonous regularity; drownings, and infant deaths in a place where there was no hope of care by a doctor. The settlers displayed a stoicism almost incomprehensible now, enduring a primitive peasant-like existence in rough huts, clearing patches in the dense, matted bush to plant vegetable gardens, suffering the vagaries of a wet climate, flooding river and the constant plague of sandflies and mosquitoes. Perhaps the greatest hardship was not physical, but mental; isolation, communication with no one but one's immediate family and a few other settlers who lived down the river or across the lake. Sometimes the men might travel up the coast or over to Wakatipu to work for a spell but the women remained behind to maintain the home and tend the children. One woman spent eighteen years at Martins Bay without leaving it and rarely moved beyond the immediate surroundings of her four-roomed wooden house.

In September 1878 Alice McKenzie's mother was expecting another child and prepared to travel by the steamer to Dunedin for the confinement. But 'when the steamer arrived, it was too rough to land a boat and, blowing her whistle, she went on her way. . . . It must have been a despairing sight for my mother on the rainswept beach.' Later in the month Daniel McKenzie set off at nearly midnight and through a savage rainstorm to fetch a woman from down river to help in the birth of the child. In the storm he was forced to abandon his boat and return alone on foot through the raging streams and saturated trackless forest. 'He waded through the front door to find a foot of water over the floor. . . . My mother's bed stood in the water, and on it she lay with her two-hour-old son. . . . The open fireplace was under water. . . . He had to use cold water to give the baby his first bath. . . . He carried each of us in turn to Mother's room to see our new brother, and I can well remember seeing her sitting up in bed with her dark, curly hair hanging over her shoulders, smiling and looking quite happy in spite of the awful surroundings. . . .'

By 1879 Jamestown was deserted '. . . and the old homesteads could soon be recognised only by the light green of the wild currant. A rose or some other bush held its own for a while, eventually to be choked out by the native growth.' To some there is an air of romance about the remote, bush-covered site of Jamestown. But the trees hide not romance, only memories of bitter tragedy, dreary hardships and, above all, the unbreakable spirit of its early inhabitants.

A handful of settlers continued to make their life at Martins Bay even after the demise of Jamestown. But numbers slowly dwindled and only the McKenzie family stayed on after the turn of the century. Daniel McKenzie's bachelor sons, Hugh and Malcolm, continued to raise cattle on the block of land on the western shores of the bay; a hard, lonely and profitless life alleviated only by the occasional visit by prospector or hunter. A track good enough for horses was finally completed up the Hollyford in the late 1880s. When the McKenzies wished to sell their cattle they had to first clear the track and prepare stockyards at halting points, and then drive their herd up the Hollyford, down the Greenstone, Mararora and Oreti valleys, some 250 kilometres to Mossburn in Southland!

The McKenzie brothers finally sold out to Davy Gunn in 1926 but continued to work for him until World War II. Gunn became something of a legendary figure in the Hollyford, droving cattle, improving the pioneer tracks, building huts until he knew the region better than any man before or since. None of Davy Gunn's exploits surpassed the lifesaving journey he made in 1936 after a plane crashed at Martins Bay and help was desperately needed for the injured survivors. In twenty-one hours he walked from Big Bay round the coast to Lake McKerrow, rowed up the lake, then rode and led his horse more than forty kilometres to the road construction camp at the head of the Hollyford, where he telephoned for another plane to pick up the survivors on the beach.

Between 1926 and 1955, when the river he had fenced with so often finally claimed him, Gunn introduced hundreds of travellers to the valleys of the Hollyford, Pyke and Cascade, taking them on horse treks of up to a fortnight, when they roughed it in the care of a great bushman. After his death, Davy's son Murray continued the treks and today maintains a motor camp, store and museum beside the Lower Hollyford road.

The road was pushed through as far as Humboldt Creek by the start of World War II, a partial realisation of century-old roading plans. Further extension would be difficult and costly and undesirable, spoiling the wild and remote character of this great South Westland valley. The Hollyford and Martins Bay area came within the boundaries of Fiordland National Park in 1960 and since then tracks have been upgraded, tramping huts established, bridges erected over creeks and rivers. And it is possible to move on the river by jetboat and travel by plane and helicopter. But none of this has diminished the breadth and majesty of river and lake, forest and wild shore. In the Hollyford the memory of Davy Gunn stands strong and on the beach at Martins Bay one will always feel the spirit of the McKenzies.

∽∞∽

The track begins where the road abruptly ends, finally hemmed by the river against bluffs at Humboldt Creek. And if the river decides to flood, the first kilometres may be impassable in the low-lying region bounded by aptly-named Eel and Swamp creeks. The hard stony tracks of the mountains are behind; boulders will not hinder the traveller here, more likely soft mud and the channels of wandering streams. The atmosphere is close and moist, insects abound; the plaintive call of the pipit is exchanged for the whoosh-whoosh of bush pigeons flying heavily through the high trees, and the kea's shriek for the parroting rattle or bell call of its bush-bound brother, the kaka.

At first there are open spaces by the river, white-flowering cabbage trees and the pendulous red blooms of tough angular flax. But the flat, easy trail is soon swallowed by the forest, edged by ferns and canopied by towering kahikatea, matai and rimu. The river is closed by the trees and channelled by the ranges that loom on either hand. The track is little more than fifty metres above sea level, but from sudden clearings on the riverbank one can see where the mountains begin to rise barely a kilometre away on either side of the river, rising so abruptly and so densely clothed by bush that their summits are hidden 2000 metres above.

This is deer country and the quiet traveller might glimpse passing shadows in the forest, even a raised head followed by its swift and silent disappearance in the confusing tangle of trees. Like most other national parks, Fiordland is divided into shooting blocks for hunters, to cater for sporting interests which help to reduce the heavy population of introduced deer that threaten the growth and regeneration of forests unadapted to browsing animals. The still warmth of the afternoon may be broken by a distant rifle shot; or more likely by the hammering drone of a helicopter with carcases slung beneath its belly, the spoil of professional meat hunters.

The track winds with the changing course of the river and, about ten kilometres from the end of the road, emerges on to the open flat of Hidden Falls Creek and its huts. Now the valley opens out towards the valley of the Pyke and the lower hills that surround the junction of the two rivers. The falls that give the creek its name are well described; a few minutes walk from the main track, they are totally obscured by rock and bush until one is almost upon them. The cascading waters have come fifteen kilometres from the Main Divide of the Southern Alps, but in this forested valley it is hard to visualise bare rock and ice.

From Hidden Falls the track climbs gently until it reaches its highest point at only 168 metres. Swamp and flooding river edge are avoided in crossing spurs of the Bryneira Range; the track becomes firm and stony, at times cut sharply into the clay, threaded by small streams. The forest becomes more open and increasingly one grows more aware of glistening ice to the west until, at Little Homer Saddle, one looks out to the chiefly splendour of Tutoko. From this point the glaciated mountain dominates the journey down valley, almost to Martins Bay.

From the saddle, down to Little Homer Creek and its 60-metre falls; back to the edge of the Hollyford and its wider blue waters strewn with the gaunt debris of past floods. Then blue gives way to black and the joining waters of the Pyke as the track meanders through forest and small clearings to Lower Pyke Clearing and its tourist lodge. Across the Pyke the view is closed by ice-carved bluffs at the end of the Skippers Range, but to the west, framed by lonely matai trees, rises the bulk of the Darran Mountains with Tutoko now tent-like and shadowed with the lowering sun. On a still, clear evening at Lower Pyke Clearing there is a dark and heavy magnificence about the scene: the oily swirl of the Pyke beneath tree-strewn bluffs, the figured green-black of the single trees on the flat and the gunmetal blue shadows of Tutoko's summit rocks beside the yellowing ice.

A quarter-hour walk from the clearing leads to Lake Alabaster, unsuspected behind the shield of forest. Kamahi lean close to the startling white beaches and circular ripples mark the rising of trout. In a stride, it seems, the closeness of the Hollyford is gone; across the lake lies the rolling hill-forest country of South Westland, the mineral-rich spurs of the Olivine Range, the valleys of the upper Pyke, Barrier, Cascade and Jackson marking the line of the Great Alpine Fault. And whether Alabaster's waters are still or rough, one remembers Barrington and his party in 1863, crossing the Pyke where it issues from the lake in a roughly constructed dugout—christened the 'Maori hen'—during their epic prospecting journey (see Routeburn chapter).

The traveller needs no 'Maori hen' now, for a high suspension bridge saves the danger of a ford, across to the slippery rock of the track beneath the bluffs. But soon the noise of Pyke rapids is left behind as the track swings through the big bush below the Skippers Range. For two hours or more there is the silence of towering tree, flaring fern and undergrowth tangled with supplejack. The soft track deadens any footfall and even the noise of chattering companions may be lost at a distance of a hundred metres. No sky, no view until, almost at the head of Lake McKerrow, the sight of the Hollyford is awesome in its powerful rapids. A normally dry channel, forming an island, testifies to the power and scope of the river in flood.

From the head of Lake McKerrow, the early settlers rowed twenty kilometres to Jamestown, a hazardous undertaking on this fiord-like lake which is made suddenly stormy by strong westerlies straight off the Tasman Sea. But the tramper follows the Demon Trail, eight to ten hours, up and down the spurs beside the lake, thinking of the McKenzie brothers or Davy Gunn droving a herd of recalcitrant cattle along the infuriating vertical meandering of the trail. There is bluff, gully, and creek after creek, the five most dangerous now spanned by wire walkways. The monotonous names of the creeks do not relieve the toil of the journey (Three Mile, Five Mile, Six Mile), only the occasional beach where one may look out to the hills across the lake. At last, a softening profusion of ferns show where the Demon Trail relents.

Just north of the Demon Trail is the Hokuri Creek and its hut. From here the track follows the stony beach where overhanging kowhai are host to bellbirds and tuis. In the last bay but one there is little to mark the site of Jamestown amid the gently drooping trees at the top of the beach. A sharp eye might detect jetty piles under calm water or an ancient struggling fruit tree; but the real evidence of settlement is the regenerated bush, lines of young trees where the land was once cleared.

The track leaves the lake and an hour or so from Jamestown the forest breaks into the clearings, river and sandhills of Martins Bay. There is still much land in private hands, passed on over a hundred years, so that huts and lodges edge the final sweep of the Hollyford to the sea or border the rough airstrip. Despite the huts and airstrip, after the long walk down the valley one feels the remoteness of Martins Bay, understands the isolation and hardship that the early settlers endured. The scene is depressing and inhospitable in wet, windy weather but admits a mysterious brooding calm when the sun drops into a settled sea, the soft beach turns gold and the white trunks and dark heads of kahikateas stand clear against the misted hills of Fiordland.

Martins Bay is a place to linger—though the sandflies demand a certain level of activity!— whether fishing in sea, river or lagoon for trout, eels, flounders, whitebait; or exploring the bush and coastline. The forest is dominated by kahikatea, miro, rata and kowhai, attracting pigeons, tuis, bellbirds and kakas; the water is dotted with ducks and swans. The northern coast is decorated by fantastically sculpted rocks and a thriving colony of barking fur seals rules Long Reef. Across the river to the south there are raking sand dunes and traces of the old McKenzie homestead, marked by wind-bent gum trees. There is no difficulty here recalling the sad figure of Mrs McKenzie, large with child, staring hopelessly through the rain as the steamer blasted its whistle and went on its way.

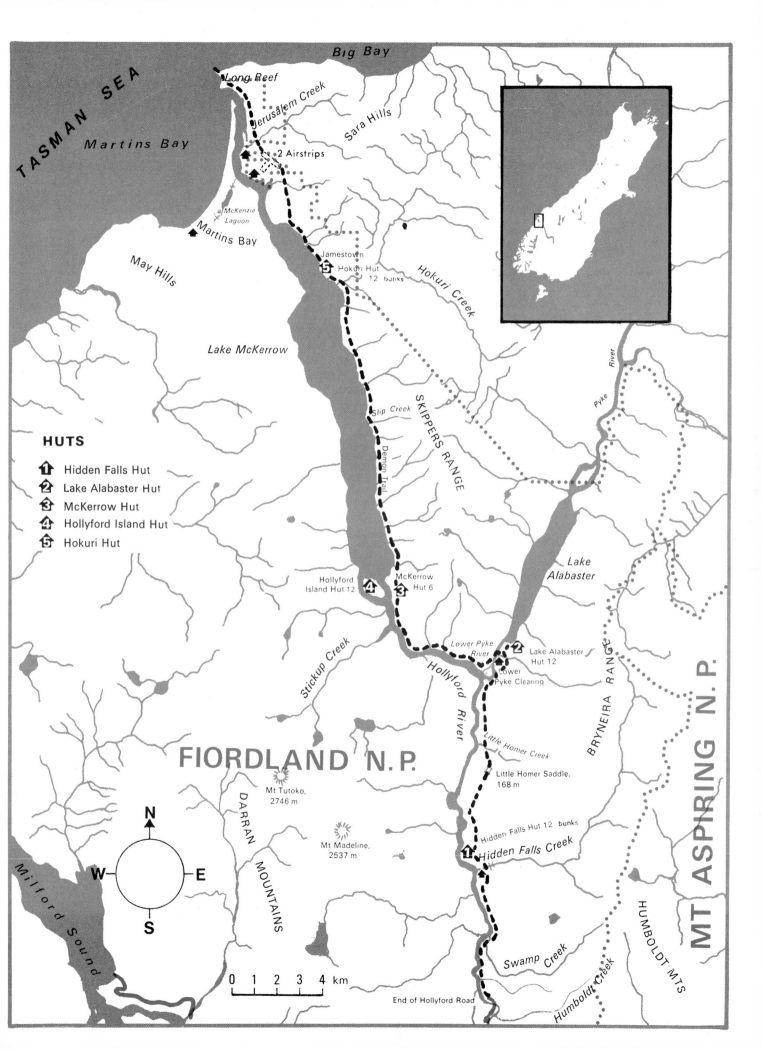

HUTS

1 Hidden Falls Hut
2 Lake Alabaster Hut
3 McKerrow Hut
4 Hollyford Island Hut
5 Hokuri Hut

Big Bay

TASMAN SEA

Long Reef

Jerusalem Creek

Sara Hills

2 Airstrips

Martins Bay

McKenzie Lagoon

Martins Bay

Jamestown

Hokuri Hut 12 bunks

Hokuri Creek

Lake McKerrow

May Hills

Slip Creek

SKIPPERS RANGE

Pyke River

Demon Trail

Hollyford Island Hut 12

McKerrow Hut 6

Lake Alabaster

Stickup Creek

Lower Pyke River

Lake Alabaster Hut 12

Lower Pyke Clearing

BRYNEIRA RANGE

MT ASPIRING N. P.

FIORDLAND N.P.

Hollyford River

Little Homer Creek

Little Homer Saddle, 168 m

Mt Tutoko, 2746 m

DARRAN MOUNTAINS

Mt Madeline, 2537 m

Hidden Falls Hut 12 bunks

Hidden Falls Creek

N
W E
S

Milford Sound

Swamp Creek

Humboldt Creek

HUMBOLDT MTS

0 1 2 3 4 km

End of Hollyford Road

South across Lake McKerrow; from Hokuri Creek

Fur seal bull at Long Reef

Rock on beach, Martins Bay

Mount Madeline from Little Homer Saddle

Martins Bay

Kahikatea near old McKenzie Homestead, Martins Bay

MILFORD

WEKA

Kea

Clinton Valley from below Pompolona

Sutherland
Falls

Head of Lake Te Anau, near Glade House

153

OF ALL the tracks in this book, the Milford needs least introduction. Since 1889, when the first tourists followed the rough track from Lake Te Anau to Milford Sound, tens of thousands have traversed what became known early as 'the finest walk in the world'. Descriptive clichés abound and experienced trampers now scorn the wide pathway, the bridges, the signs and the luxurious huts. But development and heavy use of the track have made small mark on the granite canyons and vaulting waterfalls; the track remains a tenuous path through the most unconquerable landscape in New Zealand.

The Milford Track and its facilities allow everyone to feel and understand at close quarters the scope and grandeur of Fiordland, something which can never be done from the inhibiting confines of motor coach or plane. If you have never been to Milford Sound, then avoid going there first by road. Take the four-day journey overland, up the Clinton canyon, over Mackinnon Pass, past the Sutherland Falls; the arc of rock and the line of water build a heightening sense of anticipation that is climaxed by the sudden revelation of the grandest fiord in the south.

The spectacular nature of the landscape impressed itself on the Maori and a number of legends relate the labour of the gods in hewing out the sounds and mountains. One story reveals both the Maori feeling for the scenery of Milford and their appreciation of the region's one serious drawback. The god Tu rested after his enormous exertions in hacking out Poi Poi Tane (Milford Sound). Te Hine-nui-te-po (Goddess of the Underworld) came to examine his handiwork and became alarmed at the beauty of the land he had made, afraid that men who saw it would want to live there forever. To remind them of their frailty and mortality she released a large namu (sandfly) at what is now known as Sandfly Point (Te-namu-a-Te-Hine-nui-te-po). The namu and its progeny thrived throughout the sound, so that now there is no incentive to linger, no matter how magnificent the view!

The great sound was named after Milford Haven by Welsh sealing captain John Grono in 1823. From that time the magnificent harbour was regularly frequented from the sea. But no one came to stay until Donald Sutherland sailed 100 kilometres up from Thompson Sound in 1877: 'I don't want to sound my own trumpet too much, but this is a bully run for one man in an open boat in ten hours.' Sutherland became known as the 'Hermit of Milford', establishing a three-hut 'city' from which he prospected and explored with a variety of companions. He may have been a hermit at the beginning but he became a well known character and host to hundreds of track travellers from 1890 until his death in 1919.

In 1880 Sutherland and John Mackay turned to the Arthur Valley in their search for precious minerals. The going was tough, as anyone can gauge by peering through the trackless growth on either side of the modern track. Their bushwhacking was rewarded in the middle valley by the discovery of a fine waterfall. They tossed to see whose name should adorn it. Mackay won. The valley steepened but the going became more open through beech forest growing from an often rocky floor; but days of heavy work, rain and dwindling supplies brought them to the point of retreat. They laboured up a last rise, the masking spurs of the hills fell away, and four kilometres distant they saw the slow, silent cascade of a three-jump waterfall that they were sure must exceed a thousand metres in height. There was no coin toss this time; they were Sutherland's falls.

Sutherland and Mackay's following movements may never be exactly known. Twenty-

155

Mount Pillans
from Quintin

seven years later Sutherland said that, after discovering the falls, they climbed to what later became known as Mackinnon Pass and looked down the Clinton—but thought nothing of it because it seemed to offer no route to Wakatipu, for the discovery of which they had received some official support. It is strange, however, that he did not reveal this information when a route to Te Anau was later so eagerly sought.

In 1883 artist Samuel Moreton and photographer William Hart were taken by Sutherland to his falls. They had doubted Sutherland's description of these, especially their height, which had now grown to 1500 metres! But they were clearly beyond compare in New Zealand, and the paintings and photographs which filtered back to the towns and cities undoubtedly increased the mounting pressure for a track or road to the Milford region. More and more tourists were now visiting Milford Sound by sea, to be entertained by Sutherland and to buy his stuffed bird specimens as souvenirs.

In 1888 C. W. Adams, Chief Surveyor of Otago, decided to make a reconnaissance survey of the Arthur River, find a route to Lake Te Anau and measure the height of the Sutherland Falls. Sutherland readied a track and huts up the Arthur and in September Adams's large party of eleven (including six photographers) set off. Thomas Mackenzie, M.P. for Clutha (see Routeburn chapter), and surveyor W. S. Pillans arrived in the area at the same time, also with the intention of finding a pass to Te Anau. If Sutherland had indeed already climbed to Mackinnon Pass, he was not letting on, for the explorers tried every possibility but that.

The link was finally forged, from the east, by Quintin Mackinnon and Ernest Mitchell. Mackinnon was a colourful Scot who had fought in the Franco-Prussian War, played in a record-breaking rugby team and answered to the nickname of Rob Roy. After qualifying as a surveyor in 1881 he had gone to live beside Lake Te Anau and had spent much time and effort during subsequent years in unsuccessful efforts to find routes from the lakes to the western sounds. He was convinced, however, that the Clinton Valley at the head of Te Anau was the key to Milford. With the knowledge of Adams and with government financial support he began cutting a track in September 1888, with the help of Mitchell.

Mackinnon and Mitchell took six weeks to break through the bush of the Clinton and cross the saddle at its head. Spring rains beset them continually, saturating all their clothes and supplies; sleeping and working in wet clothes gave them debilitating sores. But even after three weeks of this, when they were forced to retreat down the lake for more food and gear, they spent only one night in station beds before returning to the fray. In mid-October, as they neared the head of the valley, they decided to stop track-cutting and make a dash for the pass and join up with Adams's party in the Arthur. Dragging themselves up by tree root and tussock, they slogged over the pass in mist and rain to spend a freezing night above the bushline. But the next day they descended to Sutherland's track near the present Quintin Huts. The way was clear. The Hermit of Milford's kingdom was isolated no longer. Sutherland was put out, noting sourly that 'he could have found the track at any time if he'd wanted to do so'. He refused to call the pass by Mackinnon's name and always referred to it as Balloon Saddle.

Adams urged full development of the route as a tourist track and Mackinnon was not slow in appointing himself chief guide. Initially it was more of a bush trek than a walk, with much of the track simply a blazed route through the trees. Sutherland had built the rude Beech

Huts near the falls but Pompolona Camp consisted of a large sleeping tent with a dining room and kitchen under calico flys—not the most comfortable accommodation on what has been ironically described as 'the wettest walk in the world'. Mackinnon made Pompolonas (scones baked with fat from melted down mutton-fat candles) for tea and after a breakfast dish of 'burgoo' he took his tourists over the Pass to the Beech Huts. Primitive conditions on the track did not deter an increasing number of tourists and the first woman made the journey in February 1890. Shortly after this, young surveyor William Quill made his incredible climb of the walls beside the Sutherland Falls, discovering the lake at their source which bears his name. Adams had finally determined the height of the falls as 580 metres, a long way short of Sutherland's grand estimate, but still making them the third highest waterfalls in the world.

Government sponsored improvement of the track continued, though its operation depended on the efforts of private individuals until 1903. In that year the Government Tourist Department took over all track facilities, including the s.s. *Tawera* which had been used to ferry tourists from the township of Te Anau to the start of the track since 1898. This ship, much modified, performs a similar service even today, providing a tangible link with the early days of the walk. By 1910, through Government development and maintenance work, the track bore little resemblance to Quintin Mackinnon's expedition track of twenty years before. Mackinnon did not live to see the benched walkway, the comfortable huts and the safe bridges, for he was claimed by the waters of Te Anau in 1892. But a stone memorial signifies his pass and its plaque was unveiled by that enthusiastic explorer of Fiordland, Prime Minister Thomas Mackenzie.

The track fell into some disrepair during World War I but more and more walkers came to tackle the overland journey to Milford during the 1920s and 1930s. The track has altered and changed course after landslip and flood until, from eighty-eight years of trial and experience, the safest and most durable line has been found through the forest, beside the rivers and over the pass. Huts burned down or were blasted by avalanche, bridges were washed away and replaced. In keeping the track open, improving it to its present high standard, and in maintaining and running the huts and lodges, there have been scores of trackmen and guides and their wives who have lived and worked on the track more for the splendour of its surroundings and the conviviality of its travellers than for the employment it afforded.

At first, walking the Milford meant return over the track to Te Anau, unless one was lucky enough to time one's arrival at the sound with the departure of a passenger vessel. After 1910, more enterprising and athletic walkers could return to Te Anau via the Grave-Talbot Pass between the head of the Cleddau and the upper Hollyford. But the return journey over the track was not broken for most until the Homer Tunnel was cut. It was possible to walk through the tunnel in 1940 but motor traffic did not begin to use it until 1954. Now the pattern is familiar. Thousands of walkers annually take the launch to Glade House at the head of Te Anau; walk the easy 54-kilometre signposted track to Milford via Pompolona and Quintin lodges; cross the sound by launch to Milford hotel or hostel, and complete the circuit of their journey by bus to Te Anau. Or perhaps fly from the Milford strip to Queenstown. A far cry from Pompolonas and burgoo and Rob Roy Mackinnon with a flaming red billycock hat and gun over his shoulder, striding off to follow the blazes through the trees.

∽∾∽

From the east, the Milford Track can be reached from the Eglinton Valley over Dore Pass; but this is a full day's difficult tramp—no way for the novice and, fortunately, no way for a road. The track is effectively, and protectively, cut at both ends by water—Lake Te Anau and Milford Sound. The track is now always walked from south to north and there is no better introduction to it than the slow evening approach by launch to the head of Te Anau. The road and open country east of the lake are left behind, the waters become narrow between bushed mountains and are bounded on the west by the mysterious recesses of North Fiord and the Worsley Valley. The clouds hang heavy over the peaks and in the apparent cul-de-sac of wall and forest at the head of the lake one can imagine the barriers and problems that faced Mackinnon and Mitchell in 1888.

One's most numerous companions on the lower levels of the track—sandflies—will greet you as you step from the boat; but their annoyance is more than alleviated by the secluded charm of the Clinton River, a trout fisherman's paradise, overhung by beech trees glittering in flashes of late sunlight. From the wharf a road leads a kilometre through mossy forest to a wide grassy clearing and Glade House. From here Dore Pass can be seen to the east, the deep valleys and tributaries of the Clinton to the west, dominated by the high-shouldered bulk of Mount Anau. Mist twisting through the trees, light rain brushing the surface of the river, the deep gloom of the black forest evening—all seem to cloak the landscape with a mystery that heightens anticipation of the journey.

The track from Glade House, almost to Pompolona, sixteen kilometres away, is wide and gentle, climbing a little at the end of the day. It is wide enough for a tractor and trailer to carry hut supplies, a task undertaken by packhorses until a few years ago. The extensive use of the track by men and animals can be detected at the margins by the incongruous growth of imported weeds. But the wide vehicle track with its weeds, and the often depressing appearance of regular mile posts, are less distracting to the national park enthusiast than the constant presence of the wire and posts of a telephone line: they are an unforgivable blot on the landscape.

One can soon tune out these unwelcome encroachments of civilisation because of the sheer splendour of the track's wider environment. The forest is unblemished and the wide sweep of the river affords views across to the Neale River or back to the bumpy summits beside Dore Pass. There will be shags and whistling blue ducks on the water, wekas on the track, quiet robins on low branches and, higher, the quick squabble and chatter of yellow-fronted parakeets. A few kilometres on, the character of the forest changes in the long grove of twisted black trunks known as the Black Forest, like the petrified scene from some gothic fairytale.

Beyond the Clinton Forks the valley narrows sharply so that on arrival at the clearing of Six Mile Hut one becomes aware of the towering granite walls of the canyon. The walls are seamed with waterfalls, an unforgettable sight after heavy rain, for the high creeks have worn no gullies in the unyielding grey rock and must simply jump into space to reach the valley floor. There is more forest travelling after Six Mile and the track fringes clear river backwaters where long brown trout slide lazily over the sand. Then the forest breaks at the open scrubby reaches of Hidden Lake and the Prairie. The amazingly flat nature of the canyon floor is fully revealed here, illustrating the power of the ancient glacier that ground down inexorably through the granite. Now Mackinnon Pass is visible, like a low wall at the head of the Clinton, with its castle tower of Mount Balloon to the east.

A rocky climb through more forest brings the walker to Pompolona Hut, perched above the now rapid-strewn river, brow-beaten by the bluffs of Castle Mount. Beyond Pompolona the track is narrower and rockier, winding through scrub, ribbonwood and fuschia, and the grade steepens where St Quintin Falls may be glimpsed (or visited) across the valley. Even on a sunny day, the layers of drooping moss on the low trees testify to the drenching rainfall of the area. A few kilometres more and colourful Lake Mintaro marks the swing of the valley to the west. Soon the track crosses the Clinton, now a big creek, and begins the climb to the pass.

The graded zigzag climbs four kilometres through the last of the forest to tussock and rock and the impressive pile of Quintin Mackinnon's memorial cairn. In early summer giant mountain buttercups and large mountain daisies decorate the slopes and hollows of the long but narrow saddle which hangs as if suspended from the stout shoulders of Mount Hart and Mount Balloon: a dress circle for viewing the rock corridor of the Clinton Canyon to the southeast and the endless blue and green convolutions of glacier-carved mountain and valley to the north and west. Keas will clamour round to share lunch at the pass shelter; from the scatter of tarns, Mount Elliott and the shelf of the Jervois Glacier will catch the eye; from the northern rim of the saddle, Quintin Huts, marked by the scar of an airstrip, will seem impossibly distant, 870 metres below.

The descent from the pass to Quintin is perhaps the most trying section of the track, the steady pounding fall along a rocky surface particularly hard on those who suffer from footballer's or mountaineer's knee! There are numerous excuses to rest—the changing view, subalpine shrubs and later, when the track re-enters the bush, the sight of successive waterfalls in the staircase-like descent of the Roaring Burn. In the course of an afternoon's tramp the change is dramatic—from keas floating on a cold alpine wind to sandflies happy in the still, humid forest; from buttercups to fern tree.

Most Milford walkers spend a day in the Quintin area exploring the bush, visiting the re-constructed Beech Huts and, above all, making the pilgrimage to the three great leaps of Sutherland Falls—248 metres, 229 metres and 103 metres, flying down from Lake Quill to make the source of the Arthur River, the road to Milford Sound. Words and pictures cannot capture the power and spectacle of the falls; the thunder and unending movement of curtains of white water are almost hypnotic in their attraction and if the walker would see all the textures and subtleties of changing light on the falls he must visit them more than once during a day, at least in early morning and in late afternoon. Those who walk the track in heavy rain will find their greatest reward in a spectacle magnified by the increased flow of water.

The 22-kilometre journey from Quintin to Sandfly Point at Milford Sound is normally undertaken in one day. This downhill stage is the longest and, because a launch has to be met for the sound crossing at about four or five in the afternoon, there is little time to linger on the way. First Gentle Annie Hill, rough and slippery in places, around the western spur of Mount Elliott; then the Arthur Valley swings to the northeast and slowly opens out to Dumpling Hill and views up Diamond Creek. The track dips through forest and clearing, the sight and sound of the river dominant, fern and massive tree standing against the slopes of the Wick Mountains,

Mount Edgar and Danger Mountain. Ten kilometres down, the track crosses to the northern bank of the Arthur to the Mackay Falls and Bell Rock, upturned and hollowed by centuries of grinding water and river stones.

Now the track is crossed by side creeks in thickening forest; the mile posts are no longer metal but wooden signs carved with the images of native birds. Their real counterparts— pigeon, bellbird, paradise duck and fantail—enliven the stands of beech and rimu and the displays of flamboyant tree ferns. The track, blasted from the rock, climbs above Lake Ada and in the water below are petrified trees, drowned centuries ago during the formation of the lake. Beyond lies yet another waterfall, Giant Gate, and the last kilometres beside the lake and river to Sandfly Point.

The climax to the journey comes as the launch moves out across the water. Slowly the span of peaks and snow, waterfall and grey cliff is revealed in the wide and high spectacle of Milford Sound; Bowen Falls and the Lion, glaciated Pembroke and at last sculptured Mitre Peak shining above the black seas of the matchless harbour; the apotheosis of Fiordland.

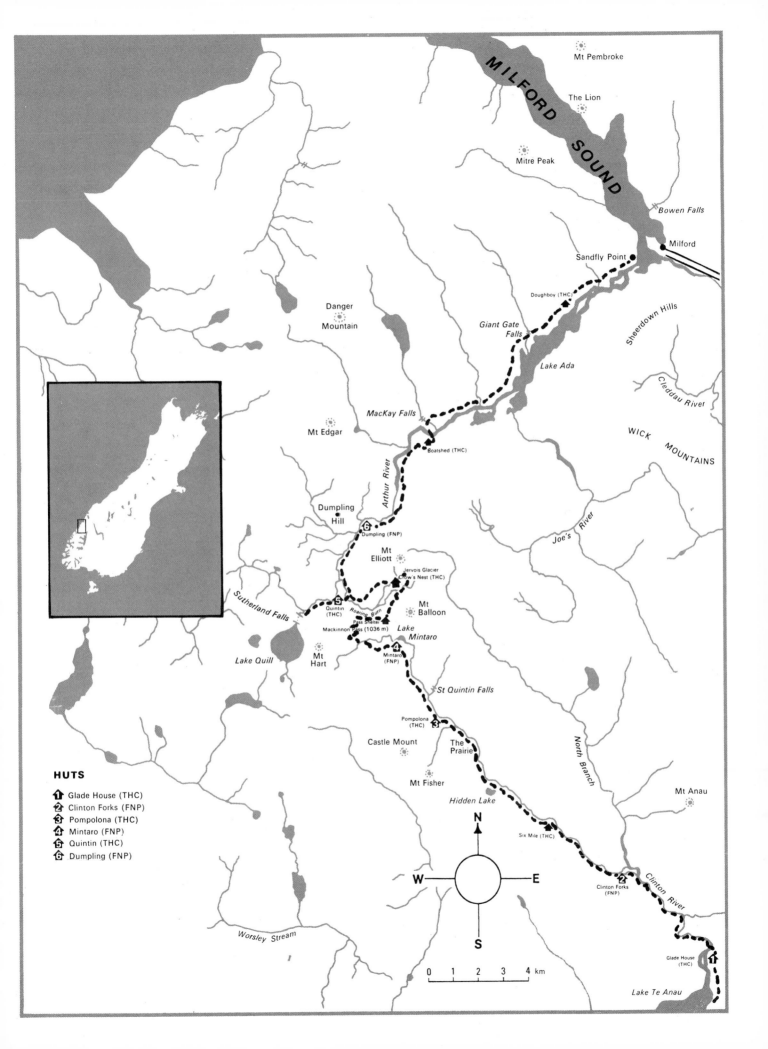

MILFORD SOUND

Mt Pembroke

The Lion

Mitre Peak

Bowen Falls

Milford

Sandfly Point

Doughboy (THC)

Danger Mountain

Giant Gate Falls

Sheerdown Hills

Lake Ada

Cleddau River

MacKay Falls

WICK MOUNTAINS

Mt Edgar

Arthur River

Boatshed (THC)

Joe's River

Dumpling Hill

Dumpling (FNP)

Mt Elliott

Jervois Glacier
Crow's Nest (THC)

Sutherland Falls

Quintin (THC)

Roaring Burn
Pass Shelter

Mt Balloon

Lake Mintaro

Mackinnon Pass (1036 m)

Lake Quill

Mt Hart

Mintaro (FNP)

North Branch

St Quintin Falls

Pompolona (THC)

Castle Mount

The Prairie

Mt Anau

Mt Fisher

Hidden Lake

HUTS

1 Glade House (THC)
2 Clinton Forks (FNP)
3 Pompolona (THC)
4 Mintaro (FNP)
5 Quintin (THC)
6 Dumpling (FNP)

Six Mile (THC)

N

W E

S

Clinton Forks (FNP)

Clinton River

Glade House (THC)

Worsley Stream

0 1 2 3 4 km

Lake Te Anau

Buttercup, *Ranunculus* sp.

White cushion daisy, *Celmisia sessiliflora*

Kotuku, *Fuchsia excorticata*

Maori onion, *Bulbinella gibbsii*

Mackinnon Pass and head of Clinton; Mount Hart above

Black Forest, Clinton Valley

Mackinnon Pass from Pompolona; Mount Balloon above

From the climb to Mackinnon Pass

Sandfly Point, the Lion and Mount Pembroke, Milford Sound

COMPANION VOLUMES BY PHILIP TEMPLE

Mantle of the Skies: The Southern Alps of New Zealand (1971)
Christchurch: A City and Its People (1973)
Patterns of Water: The Great Southern Lakes of New Zealand (1974)
Philip Temple's South Island (1975)
Shell Guides to the Routeburn, Milford, Heaphy, Tongariro (1976)
and Copland, Hollyford and Waikaremoana (1977) tracks

FANTAIL

ACKNOWLEDGEMENTS
The author extends his sincere thanks to the following people who
gave vital assistance in the compilation of this book: Les Molloy
for advice and comment on the original plan; David White for
companionship on the Copland; Ton Snelder and Jim Gilkison and
the staff of Routeburn Walk Ltd for information, travel and hut
hospitality; Jules Tapper and the staff of Hollyford Tourist and
Travel Company for accommodation, jetboat and plane; Laurie
Dennis, Eric Honey and Tourist Hotel Corporation staff on the
Milford Track for humour, company and hospitality. Especial
thanks is extended to Roy Sinclair for his work with black and white
film. Bird drawings were prepared by Jean Oates and maps by
J. Koster.

*All the author's photographs were taken with Asahi Pentax 35 mm single-
lens reflex cameras, using Super and SMC Takumar 24 mm, 35 mm, 55 mm,
and 85–210 mm (zoom) lenses. Skylight filters were used at all times, with
occasional use of yellow and orange filters for black and white photography.*